THE BIBLE
JESUS READ
IS EXCITING!!

TO
The Authors' Beloved Families
Carolyn McCall, and
Kevin and Carol
and
Yvonne Levitt, and
Mark

THE BIBLE
JESUS READ
IS EXCITING!!

*A popular introduction to the Old Testament,
featuring Scripture's "hidden plot"*

THOMAS S. McCALL, Th.D
and ZOLA LEVITT

A DOUBLEDAY-GALILEE ORIGINAL

DOUBLEDAY & COMPANY, INC.

GARDEN CITY, NEW YORK

1978

All scripture quotations are taken from the King James Version.

ISBN: 0-385-13666-8
Library of Congress Catalog Card Number 77-16850
Copyright © 1978 by Thomas S. McCall and Zola Levitt
All Rights Reserved
Printed in the United States of America
First Edition

Contents

Introduction

Obviously, the Old Testament was the Bible Jesus read. The New Testament was gradually produced after the time of Christ, so that the Messiah, His disciples and apostles, as well as all of the original Christian churches initially used only what we call the Old Testament as their Bible. All of their doctrines, all of their evangelism, and all of their practices in daily life came from the Hebrew Scriptures. Christianity was born and bred in the Old Testament.

Jesus knew and loved the Old Testament above all other books. It was constantly on His mind and its magnificent prophecies and exciting sagas rang through all of His teaching. He quoted it profusely and, in fact, in all of His recorded lessons, He never quoted any other book. The Old Testament was the continuous guide of His own life, and was understood by Him to express the very Will of God.

He never questioned its truthfulness and He considered every word—even every "jot and tittle"—to be of eternal significance. The personalities of the Old Testament were as real to Jesus as the people of His own generation, whether they lived four hundred or four thousand years before.

Oddly, followers of Jesus today—those who seek to walk in His very footsteps—do not appear to appreciate the Old Testament nearly as much as He did. To many Christians today, and many Jews as well, the Old Testament is an outmoded, cryptic, closed book. Many regard it as a collection of antiquated and superseded doctrines, events, and personalities. At worst, the Old Testament has been regarded as confusing and even at variance to authentic Christian teaching.

But rightly understood, the Old Testament is the foundation

upon which the great truths of the New Testament rest. The two great sections of the Bible are built into one complete, well-balanced structure. The Architect of the one is the Architect of the other. The Divine Author who guided the pens of Moses and Isaiah also inspired the works of the gospel writers and the apostles. The Bible, from Genesis to Revelation, is one book with one overall message—the revelation of Almighty God in a dark and blind world.

Jesus did not regard the Old Testament as merely symbolic; He lived every part of His daily life by it. He did not see its wonderful stories as mere illustrations, but as factual guides for walking with God. When He was desperately hungry for food, after fasting forty days, He quoted Moses' statement, "Man shall not live by bread alone, but by every word that proceedeth out of the mouth of God" (Matt. 4:4). All of the words that had proceeded out of the mouth of God to that time were, of course, written in the Old Testament. Whenever the Lord stated, as He often did, "It is written," He was obviously saying, "It is written in the Old Testament."

Jesus implicitly believed the voluminous prophecy of the Old Testament. He considered that it controlled events far into the future. When He was teaching about the things that would happen in the "last days" of the earth, He referred to the Old Testament prophet Daniel and assured His fascinated listeners that all Daniel had predicted would come to pass just as it was written (Matt. 24:15). He quoted the great lessons of Jonah and Noah. He reiterated the bold and bright pictures of the kingdom to come, to be found throughout the Old Testament prophets. He considered the prophetic Scriptures to be words to the wise, and He repeated them often.

Nothing could or would intervene in human history to prevent the prophecies of the Old Testament from being fulfilled, Jesus taught. He clarified many a prophecy and apparently left the scholars of Israel searching deeply into their ancient scrolls wherever He had spoken.

Jesus taught that the Old Testament predicted every important facet about Himself, the Messiah, and His mission on the earth. When He was deadlocked in spiritual controversy with the orthodox leaders of Israel, He referred them to their incomparable prophet, Moses, indicating that if they truly believed and respected Moses, they would honor Christ also, because Moses "wrote of Me" (John 5:46). He drew many a parallel to His own life and ministry from the writings of every part of the Old Testament. The healing bronze serpent of Moses was representative of the Messiah's own power to keep men from perishing and to give them eternal life. The "stone which the builders rejected," pictured by the Psalmist, was to become the "head," with reference to the Messiah's own rejection and future exaltation. He saw Himself throughout the Pentateuch, the prophets, and the poetry, and He frankly and plainly drew out the subtle meanings of the ancient writings for the overwhelmed crowds who thrilled to His teachings.

As the appointed time for His death drew near, He taught that the Scriptures were replete with references to that one-of-a-kind event. He told His stricken disciples that the Son of Man must die "as it is written of Him," and He quoted the prophet Zechariah's lament, "Smite the shepherd, and the sheep of the flock shall be scattered" (Matt. 26:24, 31).

Even His resurrection was a fulfillment of Old Testament revelation, according to Jesus. The one Messianic sign Israel was to have after the rejection of the Messiah was the "sign of the prophet Jonah"; as Jonah was in the fish three days and three nights, so the Son of Man would be three days and three nights in the earth.

And thus after His resurrection, Jesus is found with His disciples expounding the entire Old Testament as referring to both His suffering and His glory:

Then He said unto them, O fools, and slow of heart to believe all that the prophets have spoken:

Ought not Christ to have suffered these things, and to enter into His glory?

And beginning at Moses and all the prophets, He expounded unto them in all the scriptures the things concerning Himself. (Luke 24:25–27)

He went on forty days with His disciples before ascending to
His Father, according to the New Testament record. In that time,
He taught the Old Testament as no one else ever had. The effects
of this forty-day "Bible school" of Jesus were galvanizing on the
disciples. Peter, who had denied the Lord three times on the night
of the crucifixion, was able to preach the sermon that saved three
thousand people only seven weeks later (Acts 2). The other disciples were to go on to distinguished careers as apostles of the first-
century Church, all dying martyrs' deaths for the cause of salvation by their Teacher.

If we omit the Old Testament today, we are omitting 75 per
cent of God's Word. The majestic Old Testament, towering
above all other ancient literature in scope, philosophy, poetry, and
history, is truly one of the precious possessions of human heritage.
Without it, Judaism flounders, Christianity is rootless, and secular
scholarship of antiquity is in poverty. Even the non-Biblical religions, borrowing heavily, if the truth be told, from the original
Word of God, suffer by not consulting the monumental works of
the world's first Holy Writ.

For those of the Christian faith, the Old Testament is imperative. If the Founder read, taught, loved, quoted, and considered absolutely authoritative this Word of God, then surely the disciples
must do no less. To understand the utterly fascinating stories of the
Old Testament, to obtain a working knowledge of its powerful and
exciting message, and to come to know the personalities who spoke
for God and the challenging history of God's chosen nation is to
gain a greater perspective on the human condition. We will understand the person and work of Jesus Christ in an infinitely deeper
way and we will also have the privilege of seeing how we, today, fit
into that divine panoramic view of history if we are acquainted
with the Old Testament.

In a much more objective way, the Old Testament has become
increasingly applicable as a commentary on our own times. The
"last days" of the Old Testament—that period spoken of by a
host of prophets when the King will return and the world as we
know it will end its suffering—seem remarkably close, to those
who analyze the predictions of the Old Testament. A working
knowledge of the end times prophecies of the Old Testament

gives any thinking person pause today; we get the eerie feeling that the once puzzling forecasts of the ancient seers are rapidly coming into focus. If the Lord thought of the Old Testament as containing many a word to the wise in His day, we should only take that lesson all the more seriously in our own times.

Finally, the Bible Jesus read is exciting. We think you'll agree, as you progress through this book of exposition and illustration of the Old Testament stories, that the ancient Scriptures are very exciting indeed. Too few people realize the impact, the drama, the pathos, and the excitement of these ancient scrolls today.

Join us now as we look into the entire story of mankind, from the instant when God made the angels until the climactic end of the world. We guarantee it: the Bible Jesus read is exciting!

DR. THOMAS S. McCALL
ZOLA LEVITT

PART ONE

THE STORY

To the law and to the testimony: if they speak not according to this word, it is because there is no light in them. (Isa. 8:20)

. . . man doth not live by bread only, but by every word that proceedeth out of the mouth of the Lord . . . (Deut. 8:3)

1

"In the Beginning..."

There once was a "time" when only God existed.

Nothing else was "there," "anywhere." No worlds, no stars, no universes.

God existed alone, by Himself, in peace, love, and harmony.

And then one "day" God created something other than Himself. God introduced creation into what was utterly uncreated. He made things—things that were not God. From eternity with love He made our habitation, matter and energy.

He first made the angels in all their splendor, spiritual beings unlike those material beings that we are accustomed to experiencing around us. Then He made light, the celestial bodies, the earth, and all the rest of the physical universe. And finally He created that intriguing set of entities we call living things—the plants and animals, and ultimately, in His own image, man.

When He finished these mighty works of creation He evaluated what He had made. He called it good—"very good."

"THE BIBLE TELLS US SO"

The only source of the above information is the Bible, of course. Man has forever made guesses at how all we see came into being, but they have indeed been only guesses. Imaginings about our planet and its life being the laboratory experiment of superior creatures elsewhere in the universe, or beyond it; scenarios about life evolving on its own and the universe making itself, and all the other theories of origins which come and go, tend to be just that —imaginings.

The Bible addresses itself to the whole story, answering all questions for those who would believe the revelation it presents. The opening chapters of the Bible indicate that God, the beginningless One, made all the rest. "In the beginning God . . ." commences Scriptural revelation, and we are told that God has chosen to explain what happened before we came into being.

The majesty and grandeur of the opening chapter of Genesis surpasses all man-made theories of origins in its completeness and its power. It describes God as having feelings, along with His omnipotence and omniscience. The world and the universe are apparently a gift, a sublime, incredibly well-adapted gift of God to man. Life itself is a breath of God which turns dust into living, thinking, feeling existence.

God is not, according to Scripture, the Maker of a clever self-operating dollhouse of magnificent proportions, but rather the Giver of all creation. He does not stand aloof from all these proceedings, curious as to how His working model will turn out under the management of His walking, talking caretakers—mankind. Rather, He is passionately involved in all He has made, as we see immediately in His first dealings with His first man.

ADAM OF EDEN

It must have been fascinating to be Adam.

Which of us would not like to have been the very first human being, walking along through a bright new world in which every newly created thing caused great wonder and intrigue? Ever since Adam, men have universally wanted to have what he had—dominion over all the earth.

God appointed Adam King of the whole world, in effect, and informed him about its management. As an exercise of Adam's authority, the man was given the privilege of naming all the animals as they passed in review before him.

Adam must have felt immensely important as the inheritor of this priceless legacy, but he also somehow felt incomplete. After observing the entirety of God's animal creations, in all their variety, novelty, and beauty, the man still lacked something. God supplied it, from Adam's side.

No woman ever made a more dramatic entrance than Eve. Imagine Adam, now a veteran at appreciating living creatures of every conceivable kind, when he confronted the meticulously designed Eve, so perfect a companion for him. "This is it!" paraphrases The Living Bible, in an appropriate rendition of Adam's probable reaction to the first female human being.

God made Eve, we are told, so that Adam would not be lonely and so that mankind might populate the earth. Eve was perfectly compatible with Adam, emotionally, intellectually, and sexually, so that the two together "became one flesh." God "blessed them, and called their name Adam," the King James Bible translates, interestingly (Gen. 5:2).

It should be appreciated that Adam and Eve became the possessors of a very hospitable environment quite unlike that which we struggle with today. We still advisedly use the description "Garden of Eden" to express the utopian aspects of some delightful place, and Eden was a lovely and enchanting place indeed. There were no hazards involved with Eden, no tilling of the ground, no predatory animals. Adam had enough work to do to keep him from boredom, but basically all necessities of life were divinely provided for our common parents.

The happy couple ate from the crops that spontaneously appeared in the garden, enjoyed regular fellowship with the Creator, and didn't own an umbrella. The earth watered itself, cultivated itself, and generally behaved in ways that promoted the oncoming paradise that Adam and Eve's progeny were apparently supposed to enjoy for all time.

These marvelous conditions obtained during the early period in the lives of the original couple, previous to the birth of their first child. We are not aware of how long that time was but we assume it to be brief, since Eve's first pregnancy probably occurred early in God's experiment. The Almighty had made it clear that He wished to see the earth replenished.

Had it not been for a fateful event involving a less-than-honest creature in the Garden we might all still be enjoying those idyllic conditions today.

THE SERPENT AND THE TREE

Adam was not a robot; he had the privilege of choice. God had made him with a free will.

In this quality Adam was like the angels and not like the other creatures of the earth. The man did not behave by instinct, like the animals, but by choice, like the spiritual beings.

And there existed one big choice in the Garden—that forbidden tree. There was always the possibility that Adam might break God's one rule pertaining to existence in Eden, though the possibility seemed very remote. The terms were simple enough; Adam and Eve could eat from all the trees of the Garden—and there were hundreds, possibly thousands—but not from the one God called the Knowledge of Good and Evil tree. If Adam would choose to eat from the one forbidden tree, the result would be death. Rebellion against God brought death. Obviously, if Adam had not eaten of that tree he would still be alive, according to God's terms.

Now the serpent was not merely a serpent but actually an angel. The Scriptures relate that Satan, as he is later identified, had rebelled earlier against God. It was now his intention to break the fellowship between God and Adam and thus to ruin God's plans for the earth and mankind. Satan would, in effect, gain control of the earth if he could overthrow the rule of Adam, and the rule of Adam was dependent on his not exercising that forbidden-tree option. Satan's rebellion against God is as tireless throughout the Scriptures as is God's determination to sanctify mankind.

Disguised as a beautiful serpent (and Adam and Eve had as yet no reason to find snakes, or any other animals, distasteful or un-trustworthy) Satan approached the woman. God was withholding something very fine from Adam and Eve, the serpent told her. There was knowledge to be gained from eating that forbidden fruit which would make the two of them like God. Satan promised knowledge, and in fact Adam and Eve got plenty of knowl-edge; the serpent had omitted the enormity of the penalty for this disobedience, however.

That fruit (the Scriptures do not specify an apple) changed Adam and Eve permanently. They died spiritually upon tasting it, and they would now die physically because of it. Satan had won his point. God was very grieved.

The first bit of knowledge they seemed to gain was that they were naked. They covered themselves with vegetation and hid from God in the Garden.

But God came along, asking, "Adam, where are you?" Adam sheepishly confessed to being ashamed because of his nakedness and God made the interesting inquiry, "Who told you you were naked?"

It was a fair question. Had Adam ever seen a dressed animal? Did the trees wear clothes? Did the moon come out in a different outfit every night?

The awful truth came spilling out finally. Adam momentarily tried to pin the sin on the woman "that You gave me," but the die was cast. Man now had knowledge, and along with it, death and the wrath of Almighty God.

God now took action to make the best of what had become a bad bargain. Adam and Eve would have to leave the fertile Garden and they would henceforth eat by the sweat of their brows. They would find life on earth difficult now; there would be pain in the new human condition. God replaced their inadequate coverings with animal skins—creating the first animal sacrifice and apparently giving the two instruction on the principle of sacrifice and atonement for sin (we find their sons worshipping in this manner later on, at an "appointed season").

As to Satan, God announced cryptically that he would find his ultimate doom through "the seed of the woman" (Gen. 3:15). The snake, the chosen guise of Satan, would now slither on the ground and eat the dust henceforth. Spiritual warfare, still very much in evidence today, was declared.

Adam and Eve were now aliens on a hostile planet. The Paradise they had once ruled now became recalcitrant. Eve bore children, in great pain, and Adam worked hard to confront nature, formerly his most simple endeavor.

This "vale of tears" had begun.

THE CAIN MUTINY

After leaving Eden, Adam and Eve had many sons and daughters, the first of whom was a terrible disappointment. Cain became the world's first murderer, killing his younger brother Abel out of spiritual jealousy.

It was a case of disobedience again. Cain well knew what God required in the way of sacrifice for the covering of sin, but he brought the wrong thing. Both Cain and Abel believed in God; both were conscious of their responsibility to worship Him; both brought offerings to cover their sins. Surely these first offspring of the first couple to receive God's instruction on atonement well knew where the Almighty stood on sacrifices.

But Abel's sacrifice was acceptable to God and Cain's was not. Abel had brought a lamb from his flock to the altar; Cain had chosen produce from his fields.

A careful study of the passage shows that God had instructed Cain, even *after* his inadequate offering, about what was required. God discussed the importance of the animal sacrifice, the idea of blood being shed for the remission of sin. But Cain did not accept the concept and instead became full of anger against God. He took out his frustration on his brother Abel, clubbing him to death in a field.

"Your brother's blood cries out to me," God told Cain, totally repelled by the errant rebel. Cain was exiled from the care and love of his own family and sent to dwell elsewhere forever.

Abel and Cain are very much alive today in the character of mankind. There are those who receive God's teaching on the remission of sin and those who will not—and those who will not have ever despised those who will.

EAST OF EDEN

Cain was banished to "the land of Nod, on the east of Eden," and there he married and began a line of descendants. The many sons and daughters of Adam and Eve had spread throughout this territory, and farther westward, so that the race of mankind was indeed replenishing, although not always to God's liking. The Mesopotamian Valley, probably, was now well populated.

We can trace, through remarks given along with the meticulous genealogies of the Book of Genesis (chapter 5, e.g.), that the descendants of Cain inherited his tendencies of violence, hedonism, and rebellion against God.

The more reverent tendencies of the deceased Abel were continued also, however, through his replacement, Seth. The obedient Seth was identified by Eve as the son God had "appointed me instead of Abel," and throughout his line are many godly souls. Enoch was described as a man who "walked with God," and he enjoyed the honor of translation—he was taken bodily to heaven by the Lord and did not see death (5:24). Only the invariably faithful prophet Elijah, coming much later on, was to share this singular miracle with Enoch. Methuselah's heroic longevity might be a sign of his unerring faith; his line was to produce the vitally important family of Noah.

(Methuselah's nearly thousand-year lifetime has led casual readers to think that years were measured differently in the Biblical revelation, but more likely the natural conditions that then obtained better explain those very lengthy lives of the creation times. The earth, it is thought by many scientists today, might have been quite a different place before the flood—more or less a greenhouse where vapors, rather than rain, irrigated the land, and a great canopy of water vapor in the stratosphere held off the damaging, life-shortening radiations of the sun. God caused this enormous collected water to fall in the flood, inundating the earth and forever after changing its conditions drastically. In any case, men used to live a lot longer than they do now, and further Old Testament prophecy which we will discuss later on indicates that they will do so again in the future.)

Seth's line ultimately takes us to Noah and his three sons, without whose unrelenting belief in God there would be no one to write this book and no one to read it.

2

Noah Found Grace in the Eyes of the Lord

All too early in the history of man we are ready to witness the first use of a lifeboat. And what a boat!

Whatever else can be said of Noah, he was faithful. He was so faithful that he built a big boat, according to directions from the Lord, obviously having no real idea of what such a boat was for. And he obediently built it on dry land, to the universal derision of the unbelievers all around him. Men had conceivably made small craft to travel on small bodies of water, if those were in existence then, but certainly no one had ever attempted a vessel of the prodigious proportions advised by God—and so far from any harbor!

Noah must have been a source of amusement to those without a complete weather report.

FROM THE FALL TO THE FLOOD

Life on earth between the Garden of Eden and the Ark of Noah must have been immensely interesting. For one thing, due to the long lifespans, men knew their great-great-great-grandfathers (add a few greats in the case of Methuselah).

What learning must have accumulated as the younger generations constantly interviewed those who had known even the originals—Adam, Eve, Seth, Enoch. The oldsters must have shrugged in sadness over the memory of Abel the faithful, and those who had heard father Adam tell of the Garden must have become misty-eyed at the thought of what were truly "the good old days."

The wise old men must have philosophized over what might

have happened if only their original father and mother had not listened to the cajoling of the seductive Evil One of the Garden. Would they now live forever instead of eventually meeting death? Would they still enjoy that magnificent Garden? Would the whole world have become Eden for them, to accommodate all their generations? Would God talk with them as they strolled the pastoral fields and forests, as He had so often with their forebears?

That strange enemy death was with them now, however. Every one of them lived with that sad fact; however long they endured, they each departed. And the world was no Eden, it was clear. The men of the world suffered, and the animals suffered along with them.

The animals had changed. They too were expelled from Eden, which remained closed to habitation until the flood destroyed it, and they roamed the fertile earth, searching out their sustenance. Some of the reptiles reached enormous age and size and were called behemoths, or dinosaurs. Men drove them back from the settlements they established and death was the common enemy of the animals as well.

That luxurious canopy of vapor over the earth—the water above the "firmament" (Gen. 1:6-8)—still provided for a fine, even climate and a most salubrious atmosphere everywhere. Giant ferns and massive plants flourished over the globe and there were no ice caps, deserts, or otherwise infertile areas of the world. Fossil fluids buried beneath the present sands and ice-fields of today's world testify mutely to that once totally fertile earth, its life teeming generously all over the globe.

The mists that rose from the ground each day watered the vast stretches of vegetation, and though men combatted thorns and weeds, it is probable that the earth relinquished its crops more easily than it does today. Those who tilled the farms did not have to depend on capricious rains and proper seasons; no one had ever *seen* rain before the well-prepared Noah.

It is fascinating but hopeless to speculate on the character of world civilization at that time. We cannot know if there were millions of souls, or even billions; whether they lived in cities or spread out sparsely over the land; whether they had wars; whether they created static working societies or pursued high culture. It is clear in the Scriptures that the world was populated by advanced, thinking men at this time: by the end of the first six generations, man had already built cities, herded cattle, played musical instruments, and smelted brass and iron (Gen. 4:17–22). The Bible tells of no ape-like "cave men," and no leisurely evolution of the human brain. According to God's revelation those first men and women were as capable and inventive as we are today.

They were also as unmindful of God as we are today, it seems, because it becomes increasingly clear that God was not at all pleased with the progress of mankind.

THE EARTH, THE FLESH, AND THE FLOOD

Civilization was a disaster from God's point of view.

It was one great sea of evil thought and evil deed. Noah came about fifteen hundred years after the Fall and the expulsion from the Garden, and he turned out to be God's only real friend. Noah and his family were apparently the only God-fearing people to be found anywhere, and the Almighty was discouraged.

Can God be discouraged? Our finite minds grapple with difficulty over God's regret that He had ever made man. We wonder how the omniscient One can have made a society that He eventually almost totally destroyed. Man did it, of course, by exercising his free will and taking again and again the unfortunate option of Eden. God's enemy, we can safely assume, was on the scene with many offers in exchange for infidelity to the Almighty. We can only ponder such cosmic questions as the character of God and the nature of good and evil in the light that we do have. The world was inundated by a great flood by the Will of God in response to the common depravity of man, but God did not choose to destroy it all. Through Noah he continued the men and the animals of the earth. Through one family He went on with His unique experiment, man, and His ongoing warfare with Satan.

And so it was that God informed Noah that the great flood was coming. Water would pour down on the whole earth. Everything would be ruined, all living creatures drowned, except those Noah took aboard the ark.

What's an ark? Noah must have thought. How can water "pour down"? And finally the oft-repeated but grateful, "Why me, Lord?"

"Noah was a just man and perfect," the Scriptures record. He had three married sons and a wife of his own. These eight people are the ancestors of every one of us, of course, and if the Biblical record is to be taken seriously, we must be thankful for their faith.

Noah was instructed in great detail about ark-building. God left nothing to chance. The precise dimensions of Noah's ark are given and it must be appreciated that this was a big ship indeed. Its length was about 450 feet, its width 75 feet, and its height 45 feet. Durable acacia wood, found prevalently in the Middle East, was to be the basic building material. The wood was to be sealed within and without with watertight pitch.

Interestingly, modern naval authorities agree that the plans for the vessel were most apt for the circumstances. The materials and dimensions would produce an exceptionally seaworthy craft today. In this, as in a thousand other details, the Old Testament record bears up perfectly under modern scrutiny and what we have come to consider our advanced knowledge.

Building the ark was not an overnight job. Noah and his sons worked on the project for 120 years.

Now if such an undertaking were to happen today we might expect the formation of a gigantic religious boat-building movement. Considering the 120 years of preparation, one might think that at least some talk would have been generated about whether it would not be discreet for each village to construct a municipal ark. Politicians, one would expect, might have become interested, and certainly ecologists. There might be cults, with slightly different ways of boat-building, or perhaps mountain-climbing, to avoid the coming disaster.

But actually Noah was never taken seriously. He was mocked and made fun of. No one helped him in his task; no one believed him. Noah is something like the first of the disbelieved Old Testament prophets, all of whom were always right and most of whom were never taken seriously. Though he did not prophesy, per se, at that point, he must surely have been asked what he was up to. And there weren't very many ways to explain the ark other than to explain the coming calamity, after all. But somehow, no one chose to join Noah.

Perhaps Noah was a poor missionary. More likely God was only too candid when He sighed, "It repenteth me that I have made them." The human race was doomed.

As the time for the coming judgment neared, Noah began to gather the land animals, in which task he must have received considerable help from the Lord. As surely as the mysterious instinct to migrate cues the animals in their proper seasons, so they came by God's Will to Noah and his strange vessel. Seven of each clean animal and two of each of the unclean category, according to God's distinctions, approached the ark and boarded, and Noah and his sons must have rejoiced in this wondrous justification of their labors. (The ark was sufficient, it has been calculated, to hold the samples of all of the known land animals, birds, and insects and their food, but it still must have been a harrowing voyage for the skipper.)

We should realize that the forty-day rain that ensued when all of the human and animal passengers had boarded the ark was no ordinary rain. Rain was extraordinary in those times to begin with, as we have noted, but the Biblical language describing the flood is overwhelming (Gen. 7). The "windows of heaven were opened," and the "fountains of the great deep" were broken up. The earth was massively throttled with water, at least three miles deep over its entire surface! We get the feeling from the text that this incredible deluge happened very suddenly, more like with the force of a gigantic waterfall than like rain as we now know it.

The expression "windows of heaven" has interested those who follow the canopy theory. The vapor, water, or ice that was suspended above the firmament possibly plunged down upon the earth, like the greenhouse ceiling falling in. From God's point of view—from heaven—the earth would suddenly be exposed, naked to the sun and the stars, and the effect would look like a great window being opened. Hail, ice, and water must have cascaded down as the stunned Noah gazed for the first time on the full orb of the sun.

The "fountains of the great deep" have been conceived to be huge water deposits beneath the earth which might have been the source of the universal mists that had formerly watered the ground. They gushed forth water from below, as volcanos gush forth lava, and they added to the waters from the firmament above.

Of course we are speculating, since the record gives only the few stray hints we have referred to in describing this one-of-a-kind event. But it is clear that no other boat large or small survived the flood, and nobody seemed to be able to change his mind about God at the last moment and escape the judgment. Only the ark negotiated the catastrophe successfully. The waters must have come extremely suddenly upon the earth, and God had obviously made a vast change in His original model.

Noah's veritable zoo floated along for seven months while the able seamen looked in every direction for land. While the inundations had ceased in forty days, it took quite some time for all the water to subside and begin to expose the tallest mountain peaks. The ark finally came to rest of its own accord on the sixteen-thousand-foot Mount Ararat in what is now eastern Turkey, and Noah began some experimental efforts toward debarking.

He sent out a raven and it did not return, indicating that it had found some habitable resting place. He followed with a dove, and this bird returned to the ark with an olive leaf in its beak. Vegetation had survived! Life could begin anew on dry land!

A full year after the flood began the inhabitants gladly went forth out of the ark, down the mountain and into the now exposed plains. (Recent archaeological expeditions to Ararat have returned with tantalizing hints that the ark survived the past five thousand years, perhaps encased in ice. Photographs of some dark object, seemingly always out of reach of the climbers, and pieces of allegedly carved wood have come out of such missions, but thus far no one has brought down a substantial part of a boat. That would surely be the archaeological find of all history!)

A grateful Noah was joined by his family in sacrificial worship once they alighted on *terra firma*, and God responded with a promise that there would never be another global deluge (Gen. 8–9). God showed Noah the first rainbow and indicated that it would forever be the sign of His promise. In earlier times the rainbow would not have been seen, since the sun would not have shone directly enough through the canopy to refract it. But now Noah saw that inspiring celestial manifestation we all still appreciate today; who can fail to see the great hope in the rainbow?

THE NEW FIRST FAMILY

Noah, rather like Adam, inherited the earth. With his little family he began to till the ground, finding the world still a hospitable place. There had been some changes, of course, but basically human and animal life continued as before.

In the course of time Noah planted a vineyard and reaped a harvest. He drank the fruits of his labors and immediately discovered something which may have been an entirely new function of the remade world. The wine had fermented; Noah got drunk.

Drunkenness was previously unknown in the Biblical record, and conceivably fruit juice did not behave the way it does under post-flood conditions. But in any case, Noah, the choice of God, lay in a stupor, naked, after sampling his fields.

His sons reacted in different ways—Ham ridiculed his father's condition, but Shem and Japheth respectfully covered their father's nudity (Gen. 9:20–23). They did so in a manner in which they would not look upon their father's exposed body, approaching him backward and laying a garment over him. The scene is heavily symbolic of that original nakedness that so troubled Adam after he had eaten of the forbidden fruit, and the covering made for him by God.

At any rate, when Noah revived he uttered a pronouncement upon his sons that God was pleased to elevate to the status of prophecy. It contained three parts:

1. In Ham's line, the people of Canaan were cursed.
2. Shem, whose name means "the Name," was blessed. He became the father of the Semites, later known as Hebrews and Arabs. All recorded knowledge about God has come down to us through this line.

3. Japheth was told that his line would prosper and dwell in the tents of Shem. He fathered those who settled the European nations.

A very lengthy genealogy follows in which a great many names found later in the Biblical record appear (Gen. 10). Some analysts have tried to reconstruct world history and the migration of peoples after the flood back to the original forebears and their descendants. God tended, throughout the Old Testament, to utilize the names of the original descendants of the sons of Noah when speaking of the various peoples of the world, and those names are often found in Gen. 10 (compare Ezek. 38:2, 6 with Gen. 10:2–3).

And indeed, if the Biblical record is to be believed, we all belong to either Shem, Ham, or Japheth.

THE FIRST SKYSCRAPER

Fascinated by the heavenly bodies, which, according to the theory of the fallen canopy, were now in view for the first time, men began to construct a tower to worship the stars. Apparently Noah's descendants continued in the old tradition of failure to worship God in the prescribed ways, and they instead purposed to create this massive pagan structure with which God was not at all impressed.

God had wanted Noah's progeny to migrate throughout the earth, but they instead seemed to congregate in the Tigris-Euphrates Valley area, where they established many cities. Apparently their building skills had progressed to the point where they were equal to the task of making a tower to "reach unto" heaven, as the King James Version renders it—or, more likely, to provide a special sanctuary where they might worship the celestial lights. (They were better astronomers than to think their tower could actually reach heaven; they built, it seems, something more like an observatory where they might be surrounded by the panorama of the night sky and thus be struck with the majesty of the Creator's works. Worshipping the works, rather than the Creator, however, is Biblically the very definition of all idolatry.)

Perhaps the tower was decorated with a giant zodiac; the pseudo religion-science of astrology might have begun here.

In any case, God put a stop to the prodigious project in a way that forced the intended migration of human civilization; He caused the builders to begin speaking different languages. Suddenly all work stopped, as the bricklayers failed to understand the hewers of timber and the foremen of the painters spoke gibberish to his crews. Confusion (in Hebrew, Babel) reigned at the site of the architectural and pseudo-religious marvel. The Tower of Babel was never completed, it seems, and the huge force of workmen and their families parted company. Each must have gone off with those few among whom some common language could be found, and so mankind finally migrated to populate the known world. The Tower of Babel has ever been the symbol of confused, polyglot paganism, separater of men from each other and from God (Gen. 11).

So now men were divided into distinct linguistic and cultural groups. The record continues with a genealogy of the descendants of Shem, the faithful son, which takes us into Mesopotamia, and a city of the Chaldees called Ur.

There is a hint in the Scriptures that the land also divided at this point. Gen. 10:25 states that during the time of Peleg, a descendant of Shem, "was the earth divided," so that the continents conceivably came into being. The "continental drift" theory—that the eastern and western hemispheres once split and slowly drifted apart—may be identified in this verse.

Thus, the human race and its culture continued to develop for some time following the flood and the Tower of Babel. In many ways the earth was in as much rebellion against God as it ever had been, but God had conceived a new plan that He was about to unveil.

The idea of redemption was to be revealed.

Men had not responded well to God's previous procedures—they just never seemed to choose God in any significant numbers—but they might well respond to being "reclaimed," as it were, by a new method of God's. God would not now destroy the world, but rather He would take steps to redeem men from their ungodliness.

Redemption is a painstaking process. The rest of the Bible, Old Testament and New, is devoted to it.

It begins with the remarkable personality who came to be known as Abraham.

3

Get Thee Up and Go:
Abraham of Ur

He is called in the Scriptures "the friend of God."

Through him is established a new kind of communication between God and man, aimed toward the redemption of the human race.

It is as if God looked down once again, as he did at the time of Noah, and selected a man to carry things on. But this time the man was not merely to survive and go on as he was in the worship of God. This time the man was to be the founder of a new kind of people—a chosen people—and the forebear of all human beings of true faith.

Abraham was the new beginning of what we now regard as redeeming belief in God, a *saving* faith. He was the father of the Jewish people and the father of *all* believers, who are later to be called "the seed of Abraham."

Abraham is truly the beginning of the end for Satan and his curse upon the human race—death.

UR OF THE CHALDEES

Abraham was not originally Jewish, a point usually missed by casual readers of the Scriptures. Actually he was a cultured, apparently well-educated product of a thoroughly pagan society which thrived four thousand years ago near the Persian Gulf.

It should be appreciated that archaeology now becomes equal to the task of verifying the complexities of the Biblical record, so that from here on we speak with confidence about names, places,

and dates. Ur, a huge metropolis of the ancient world predating
the great ages of Greece and Rome by millennia, has been exca-
vated very completely, and stunned scholars have discovered a
humbling fact—men were very advanced, very sophisticated, long
before we ever supposed.

A great library has been found in the diggings at Ur, as well as
clay tablets bearing the records of thriving commerce, literature,
and religion. Foundations of huge structures—homes, palaces, and
public buildings that rival those we make today—have overwhelmed archaeologists at that ancient site. A great civilization of
thinking, feeling human beings existed here; we no longer accurately look back on our past with condescension.

Ur was situated in the fertile area between the Tigris and
Euphrates rivers in what later became known as Babylonia. At the
level of digging which represents Abraham's time—c. 2000 b.c.—
an impressive level of cultural advancement becomes obvious. In-
dustry thrived, a nine-story pyramid-like stone temple called a zig-
gurat dominated the skyline, and actual classrooms have been
found. Perhaps the young Abraham sat in one of those very
schoolrooms mastering the peculiar wedge-shaped alphabet called
cuneiform. Slabs of clay bearing the work of the students and professors of Ur are extant, and all we lack to complete the picture of
what may have been one of the Big Ten universities of the ancient world are varsity sweaters and pennants with the legend
"Onward Ur."

The people were very religious, and Ur was likely a spiritual
center of the river valley. But they were pagan. It is clear that they
worshipped idols, raising monuments to varied gods of wood and
metal. Their priesthood offered human sacrifices, certainly never
demanded by the Almighty in heaven, and paid much obeisance
to the stars and the planets. Legend has it, though it is not
certified in Scripture, that Abraham's father Terah was deeply involved in the paganism of Ur, and in fact was a craftsman who
manufactured idols.

That infamous Tower of Babel, thrown down by the disheart-
ened God of creation, somehow had left its taint on the people
of the great Mesopotamian Plain, and visible gods—stars, statues,

and the like—were still widely preferred to the patient but silent Father above.

"DEPART!"

Out of this heathen, worldly, materialistic milieu, God chose Abraham. His name was really Abram at the start, but God was to change it in accordance with His plans for this uniquely obedient servant (Abraham means "Father of Many Nations").

God told him to leave, to get up and go, to get out of Ur and all that it represented. The territory was apparently not spiritually salvageable—God wanted Abraham to begin anew in a distant land. The coastal Canaan was the Lord's preference.

A man of firm faith, high intellect, and worldly cunning emerges as we study the remarkable career of Abraham, the choice of God. He was obviously educated and capable, physically strong, and of a willing pioneer spirit. His very obedience to the inconvenient call of the Lord has ever stood as an example to those wrestling with the Will of God. God said "Depart," and Abraham departed at once. The true descendant of Shem in his heart, Abraham could not but obey his God.

God's call included a wonderful promise to Abraham which few of those with even a modest belief in the Creator could resist. In God's words:

Get thee out of thy country, and from thy kindred, and from thy father's house, unto a land that I will shew thee:

And I will make of thee a great nation, and I will bless thee, and make thy name great; and thou shalt be a blessing:

And I will bless them that bless thee, and curse him that curseth thee: and in thee shall all families of the earth be blessed. (Gen. 12:1–3)

Thus fortified, Abraham and his kinsmen began their arduous and circuitous journey to the Mediterranean coast. They took the "fertile crescent" route through the arid terrain, still the preferred itinerary since it includes fresh water. The party of wanderers included Terah, Abraham and his wife Sarah, and Abraham's nephew Lot.

Terah did not survive the journey. He died at Haran, a town about halfway along the thousand-mile pilgrimage. Abraham buried his 205-year-old father there and resumed his sacred journey. (Lifetimes had considerably shortened since the earlier days, but were still very generous by our standards. Abraham, called in the prime of his life, apparently, was 75 when the journey commenced. He was to die at age 175.)

God was to continue to enhance and clarify his covenant with the obedient Abraham (as He was to do throughout the rest of the Scriptures, and is continuing to do today). When the faithful sojourner arrived in Canaan the Lord constantly reiterated His promises, and in final form they include the *land* (Israel), a special "*seed*" (in the language of the Garden of Eden) or progeny, and that overwhelming *blessing*. The land promise is seen fulfilled today; the "seed" referred to Abraham's descendants, and especially to the Redeemer to come, as we will further explain; the blessing accrued to Abraham's family, all of his descendants, and finally to all who, like Abraham, follow the special call of God. The rest of the Bible—the rest of human history, it is fair to say— concerns the outworking of those momentous promises God made some four thousand years ago.

ABRAHAM THE NOMAD

Abraham didn't really "settle" in Canaan when he arrived. He was more of a wandering cattleman. He was a tent dweller, moving with his herds up and down the land as a pilgrim and a stranger. He might be roughly compared to today's Bedouins who live much the same life of constant movement. Like shadows on the sands they appear and reappear today in Israel, having few possessions and leaving no trace of their brief stays in any locale.

The area of Bethel (House of God) appears in the Scriptures now as a holy place where Abraham chose to worship the Lord. It will be mentioned time and again as the Scriptural saga unfolds. Some fifteen miles north of Jerusalem, it maintained its character of holiness (or, in the later days of the divided kingdoms, *unho-liness*) for millennia.

"HAVE YOU MET MY SISTER?"

A great famine came to the land of Canaan during Abraham's time and he chose to migrate to more hospitable Egypt.

This involved a serious problem, according to the Biblical record. It seemed to Abraham that the Egyptians might covet his beautiful wife Sarah, apparently an uncommonly desirable woman. The immigrant Abraham thought that the Egyptians might do him in altogether in order to appropriate his wife, and possibly these were the customs of the times.

Thus Abraham, whose name is virtually synonymous with faith and righteousness, invented a little white lie. He insured his own safety by advising Sarah that she was to say she was his sister, not his wife. Who could have anything against the *brother* of a tempting female, after all? The yarn wasn't entirely untrue since Sarah was actually Abraham's half sister (see Gen. 20:12), but it was far from the whole truth.

Abraham's estimations of his wife were more than fair; the attractive Sarah became highly recommended in Egypt. In fact, she was recommended as a fitting wife for no less a personage than Pharaoh himself!

Pharaoh was accustomed to marrying whomever he pleased, of course, and he was quite taken with the Mesopotamian beauty. Cultivating the "brother" of the bride-to-be, Pharaoh proved a tactful and generous suitor, giving Abraham a considerable amount of valuable livestock. Sarah was installed in the royal palace where her good looks might cheer the sovereign's court on a daily basis.

God was not pleased, it goes without saying. Had He not already announced His magnificent intentions toward Abraham's line? Were not the wonderful promises accruing to the Hebrews, and ultimately the whole world, based on the "seed of Abraham" by his rightful wife? Was the friend of God going to actually give Sarah away, and even accept a reward?

We might not be surprised to see Abraham smitten on the spot by the rightfully indignant Creator, but instead His wrath descended upon the royal palace. A plague, unnamed but very grave, fell upon Pharaoh and his court, and the intelligent ruler of Egypt began to suspect that something was spiritually the matter in the royal house. The superstitious Pharaoh may not have had a clear idea of just what god was responsible for his troubles, but he could very well date the woes from the arrival of the mysterious brother and sister from far-off Ur. Genuinely afraid of the evil visitations upon the palace, Pharaoh made inquiry of Abraham and finally the truth came out.

Shocked and morally wounded, the King banished Abraham and Sarah from Egypt, letting his intended brother-in-law keep the cattle and the other possessions he had accrued in his favored status. Pharaoh granted safe conduct to the couple but made certain that he had seen the last of them. Abraham left at once, taking his cattle, silver, and gold and all the rest of the King's largesse, and returned to Canaan with his wife.

The scene is one of the very curious stories in the honest chronicles of Israel. Here is Abraham, to whom God Himself had spoken, being ordered out of a pagan land by a heathen King. The behavior of the friend of God had proved beneath the standards of the sun worshippers of the Nile. If God had grieved at the murderous jealousy of Cain, if He had been hurt by the excesses of the tower makers of Babel, if He had repented of ever making man in the first place, what must He have thought now? No man had a brighter future than Abraham, and yet, in the very spirit of the disobedient Adam himself, Abraham had done that which was obviously forbidden.

But the patient Jehovah was to continue His covenant through it all, probably glad to see His errant sojourner back in the land of Canaan. Some Scriptural analysts have taken Abraham's degeneracy in Egypt as a symbol of what becomes of men when they do not obey God to the letter. Abraham did choose to leave the land God promised to him in favor of more fertile pastures elsewhere, after all, and Egypt, in all its pagan ways, has long been taken to be the very essence of unbelief.

Whatever the case, the newly wealthy couple returned to the

land with their herds, and of course with Lot, who was ever by his uncle's side. Nothing is said of Lot in the Egyptian episode, but he now re-enters the story of Abraham dramatically, back in Canaan.

It seemed that Lot had come by some herds as well, and now the miserly pasturelands of central Canaan were not adequate for the spoils of both uncle and nephew. They decided to split up, with Abraham remaining in the mountainous central area and Lot choosing to go eastward along the Jordan River valley. Abraham established his tents at the Oaks of Mamre, which has come down to us as modern Hebron, some twenty-five miles south of Jerusalem. Lot, seeking fresh-water springs at the south end of the valley toward the Dead Sea (Gen. 13:10), made the momentous decision of settling near the infamous and ill-fated city of Sodom, about thirty miles away.

Lot was to become seduced by the celebrated debauchery of Sodom, and her sister city Gomorrah, and finally to take up residence in the former. This move would prove his spiritual undoing.

THE FIRST ENTEBBE

Lot's choice almost proved his physical undoing as well. He had selected a border city along the West Bank (still in contention to this day!) and the invaders came as faithfully as they do now.

Abraham's old countrymen, the Mesopotamians, had organized a raiding force, with the armies of five city-state Kings participating. They fell upon Sodom and Gomorrah, meeting with little resistance from the distracted night-lifers, and sacked and looted both cities. Lot was captured, along with many other citizens, and was taken northward along the river route to Mesopotamia.

The invaders were heading toward Damascus but camped, with their prisoners, at Dan, in far north Canaan. They probably assumed that they had put enough distance between themselves and the main populace of Canaan, in the central highlands, but they had not reckoned with the guerrilla fighter Abraham.

In a night raid, not unlike that at Entebbe, Abraham and his small band of 318 herdsmen attacked the totally surprised Mesopotamian army and rescued both the prisoners and the booty. The disorganized Mesopotamians were decimated and fled all the way back to Damascus, in a stunning presage of modern Golan Heights fighting.

Thankful to God for what must have seemed like a real miracle, Abraham next met with the mysterious King-Priest of Salem (later Jerusalem), called Melchizedek. Abraham paid Melchizedek one tenth of the recovered booty as an offering to the "Most High God," and then returned the former prisoners and their possessions to the Dead Sea cities.

Melchizedek is a fascinating, even mystical personality. While God was calling Abraham to procreate the Chosen Nation, He had other men in the world, like Melchizedek, who were worshippers of the true God during this patriarchal era.

Another was Job, a man God was so confident of that He "bet" Satan that no matter what the Evil One did to Job, the righteous patriarch would remain faithful to God (Job 1:12). Satan took the Lord up on the proposition, and threw the book at Job—took his possessions, killed his seven sons, and gave him a horrible disease of running boils and sores, like elephantiasis. Job bore up under the massive attacks, and only complained that he couldn't understand why God was allowing all this to happen. He had three friends who tried to persuade him that he was being punished for his sins, but Job knew better.

Finally, after a dramatic confrontation with the Lord, Job was convinced that the Almighty knew what He was doing, and that he could trust the Lord's wisdom even if he couldn't really understand why the righteous suffer calamities. After the ordeal, Job's health, possessions, and even his children were restored. He was indeed found faithful, like faithful Abraham. His ultimate conclusion: "Yea, though He slay me, yet will I trust in Him!"

"LOOK NOW TOWARD HEAVEN"

Through all of their adventures Abraham and Sarah remained childless. Somehow, despite the promises of God concerning Abraham's seed, the supposed patriarch was blessed with no issue.

Abraham contemplated the situation for some years, holding his peace. But one starry night, while he was communing with God, it all came out. "What wilt Thou give me?" Abraham demanded bitterly, "seeing I go childless." The friend of God feared that his sole heir might have to be his faithful foreman, Eliezer of Damascus, rather than his own offspring (Gen. 15:2–3).

But the Almighty reassured Abraham about his coming heir, and added that the descendants of Abraham would ultimately multiply wonderfully: "Look now toward heaven, and tell the stars, if thou be able to number them: and He said unto him, So shall thy seed be."

It was difficult for the octogenarian to trust such a promise, things being as they were, but the significant verse Gen. 15:6 relates simply, "And he believed in the Lord; and He counted it to him for righteousness." Two thousand years later the apostles of the New Testament were to seize upon this pristine expression of faith and proclaim it to the world as the very essence of right relationship with God. Man believed and God thus declared him righteous, and in that uncomplicated exchange lay the heart and soul of the New Testament.

God went on to reveal to Abraham at this point two extremely significant prophecies. First, Abraham's descendants would leave the Promised Land and live in affliction as strangers in another land for four hundred years; then they would return. This was fulfilled in the Egyptian sojourn when Israel was held in slavery for four centuries, and in the resulting Exodus under Moses. Second, and most important, God now indicated the boundaries of the Promised Land, an issue under much discussion, to say the least, today. Israel was to be bounded on the south by the "River of Egypt" and on the north and east by the Euphrates. The Mediterranean Sea, of course, marked the western border. (The River of Egypt has been understood by some as the Nile, but later Scriptures appear to designate it as the dry river bed in the Sinai known today as Wadi el Arish, not far from the present Israel-Egypt line in occupied Sinai.)

Israel has never achieved these generous boundaries, though the borders of Israel have always been a matter of military contention, as they are at present. This Biblical land grant (Gen. 15:18) has become a modern political issue of the highest sensitivity.

But the years continued to drag by with no child for Abraham and Sarah. Undoubtedly Abraham discussed the promise of God with his aged wife, with more than a little implication that Sarah was to blame for their barrenness. Sarah ultimately said that Abraham should take her maid, Hagar, and conceive his son with her, a plan not unheard of in middle eastern culture of that time. Abraham took Hagar as his concubine, not consulting God about it, and the plan, such as it was, bore fruit. The eighty-five-year-old Abraham was potent, true to God's word, and Hagar was soon with child.

But now Hagar was less satisfied to be merely a lady's maid in the household, as we might well imagine. She threw up to Sarah her own fertility and her special ability to provide for the wishes of the master. The situation between the two women grew unbearable.

Sarah received Abraham's permission to discipline her headstrong maid and Hagar ran off as a result. Pregnant, she fled through the arid country south of Abraham's encampment at Hebron, finally resting at a Negev oasis.

At this point the Lord intervened. Doubtless displeased with the triangle Abraham had created, God still respected the unborn child of Hagar as the "seed of Abraham." An angel instructed Hagar to return to her employers. Her son would be called Ishmael and he and his descendants would be unruly and abrasive against the rest of mankind, the angel prophesied. (Ishmael means "God hears"; Hagar means "refugee." The prophecy about Ishmael, the father of the Arabs—"And he will be a wild man; his hand will be against every man, and every man's hand against him"—has seemed to be realized throughout Arab history, and perhaps most emphatically in this day of OPEC; see Gen. 16:11–12.)

Things settled down for a while in the cattle-ranch country around Hebron, and Ishmael grew to be fourteen years old before God made His next step in His plan of redemption. God now moved to create a special sign of the covenant between Him and His coming chosen people. Reiterating and embellishing all the promises He had made to Abraham, God now bade him, "Every man child among you shall be circumcised" (Gen. 17:10–11).

This peculiar physical sign would henceforth identify the people with whom God had made a covenant relationship. Each male child would have his foreskin removed on the eighth day after birth—an excellent sign of Biblical accuracy, the eighth day being medically the optimum time for such surgery in view of blood coagulation capability and infection-fighting constituents. Abraham received his new name at this point also; it was becoming more obvious that the Father of Many Nations was at last to be a father through his legitimate wife.

BIRTH OF A NATION

Sure enough, Sarah became pregnant and Isaac, the first Jew, came into the world.

To say that he came as a surprise to Abraham would be to doubt the repeated promises of God, but the proud father had been a very skeptical believer on this particular matter. There was plenty of advance preparation for this important birth in addition to the previous covenant; Sarah's name was changed from Sarai (Sarah means "Princess"), and Abraham was informed shortly ahead of the pregnancy that this ultimate promise was now to be fulfilled.

But the ninety-nine-year-old one just couldn't take God seriously this time; as a matter of fact "Abraham fell upon his face and laughed." More seriously he entreated God, "O that Ishmael might live before thee" (Gen. 17:16–18).

We can sympathize. Abraham had waited a long time. He had been faithful, in his way, and he had tried everything to promote God's promises on his own. He had an heir, after all, even though the conception was tainted, but now, exhausted in his faith, he could but say to God, in effect, "Can't You just settle for Ishmael? He's *here* and he's *mine!*"

God was understanding and took Abraham's frustration in all good humor. He not only repeated that Sarah was to bear a son but He now commanded that this son be named Isaac, meaning

"Laughter." Because Abraham had laughed at the promise of God he would now go through life being reminded of this indiscretion. We can well imagine him later calling Isaac for dinner: "Laughter, come in now," and all the while muttering to himself, "What came over me that day! I'll never laugh at God again!"

Sarah was also informed of the impending birth well ahead of her pregnancy, and she was guilty of the same incredulous reaction. On this occasion three mysterious "men" visited the tent of Abraham and he greeted them with obeisances, seeming to sense their supernatural qualities. "My Lord . . . pass not away," Abraham said in salutation, and he bade Sarah to prepare them a meal. As she worked in the kitchen area Sarah overheard the conversation of Abraham and his guests, which contained the news about Isaac. She couldn't help laughing audibly. One of the strangers, now called "the Lord" (Gen. 18:13), asked Abraham why Sarah laughed at this good news. "What does your wife find so funny?" we can almost hear Him asking, as the flustered Sarah entered, trying to deny that she had laughed. Then "the Lord" reiterated the promise about Isaac to Sarah, and thus the arrival of the child called "Laughter" was surrounded with this mixture of belief and unbelief, and some misplaced mirth.

The three visitors had more to say than that, however, and the news was grave. God had run out of patience with the ways of the West Bank cities; Sodom and Gomorrah were doomed. Abraham, fearful for the safety of his beloved nephew Lot, strikes up an incredible dialogue with God in which he argues for the deliverance of the cities in which at least a few righteous ones may be found. Desperately and fearfully he pleads with God for the lives of perhaps fifty—and if not, then forty—and if not, then maybe just thirty, and so on. He moves God to declare that if, finally, just ten good men could be found, the Almighty would not destroy the cities. (Unbeknown to Abraham, the argument was hopeless. There were not ten righteous men to be found throughout the two large citadels.)

Angels came to Lot as well, as the story goes on, bidding him to consult his sons, daughters, sons-in-law, and so forth about the impending disaster. Will they believe him? Has he managed, in his time in the midst of the Dead Sea debauchery, to persuade even his own family to fear God?

The ending is known only too well, by all Bible readers. Lot is not taken seriously at all. He escapes only with his wife and two daughters as God's vengeance obliterates the two cities. And then Lot's wife disobeys God by looking back at the conflagration; she is turned into a pillar of salt.

SIBLING RIVALRY

Back at Hebron things were very joyous, at least up to a point. Isaac was born a happy baby who laughed all the time, continuing the Lord's little joke, and Abraham and Sarah were most pleased.

Ishmael, formerly the only child, of course, was not nearly so pleased. It happened that the proud parents threw a party to celebrate the weaning of Isaac when he was about a year old, and the envious Ishmael "mocked" the infant, according to the record (Gen. 21:9–10). How one successfully mocks a baby is not clear, but Ishmael's attitude of resentment made things very difficult in the complex family of Abraham.

Sarah finally declared that she had seen enough of Hagar and her obnoxious teenager to last her a lifetime. She threw a real tantrum about the whole matter and said that Hagar and Ishmael had to leave. Abraham was confused and hurt; Ishmael was *his* son, after all, and though the tent was getting a bit small for the extraordinary personalities who were now trying to live together, he was loath to see his "step-family" cast out. He consulted the Lord, but God sided with Sarah.

God said it would be best if Hagar and Ishmael left. He reiterated His covenant, making it very clear that it was to proceed through Isaac, not Ishmael (Gen. 21:12), but that He would certainly not forget Ishmael (Gen. 21:18).

Thus the rivalry between the Arab nations and Israel began quite a long time back. It actually began at a weaning party about four thousand years ago.

"THINE ONLY SON!"

We can imagine Abraham's feelings when God requested the sacrifice of Isaac!

It was some years later—Isaac was probably an adolescent—when God asked for Isaac as a "whole burnt" offering (Gen. 22:2). Abraham was to kill and cremate his long-awaited heir.

The aged friend of God did not turn his back on this command. Remarkably Abraham obeyed without hesitation. He "rose up early in the morning," and without telling Isaac the terrible consequences of God's Will, routinely gathered his materials for his usual burnt offering oblations. He took the boy and two servants and set out for the mountain in Moriah designated by the Lord.

But what about God's promises? The Almighty had specifically stated that Isaac was to be heir to the magnificent covenant; how could He now ask for the death of Isaac?

The New Testament indicates that Abraham was convinced that God would raise Isaac from the dead in order to fulfill His promises (Heb. 11:17–19). The writer of the Epistle to the Hebrews utilizes Abraham's display of perfect faith with great force by citing this terrible test from which the patriarch did not shrink.

God stayed Abraham's knife at the last moment that day on Mount Moriah (later to become the Temple Mount of Jerusalem) and a ram was substituted for Isaac in sacrifice. God was immensely pleased with the unquestioning obedience of His good servant; triumphantly He repeats still again the perpetual covenant He has made with Abraham and his seed (Gen. 22:16–18).

And so Isaac reached manhood, living in peace with his parents and not taking a wife until relatively late in life. When Isaac was 37, and Abraham 137, Sarah died peacefully and was buried at Hebron in the strange country where she had dwelt so long.

Sarah had been the most faithful of wives, following her husband to distant lands, living in tents as a nomad, tolerating the situations in Egypt and with Hagar and Ishmael, and finally giving birth to Isaac, the rightful seed of Abraham and possessor of the convenant of God.

A touching scene ensues when Abraham purchases a burial site for his beloved wife, in the land which he actually owns by the Will of God. "I am a stranger and a sojourner with you," he tells the owner of the site. "Give me a possession of a burying place with you, that I may bury my dead . . ." (Gen. 23:4). Abraham paid four hundred shekels of silver for his burial plot, and from that time on the town of Hebron has been a shrine to the Jewish people.

Abraham now longed to see Isaac married, but the devout heir had no interest in the idolatrous women that populated the territory of Canaan. A wife had to be found for Isaac, of course, so that his father could see the precious covenant continue, but where to find her?

There had been news over the years from Abraham's brother Nahor in Haran; that branch of the family had children and grandchildren. Abraham sent a trusted servant to look over the situation at Haran with a view to finding a suitable blood relative for Isaac to marry.

This servant, unnamed and unheralded, went about his sacred responsibility with a fine sense of duty and a prayerful reliance on the Lord. He asked for God's guidance on choosing the right wife for Isaac and determined that he was to choose the woman who would assist with the watering of his camels.

Thus it was that the kind Rebekah, the very soul of hospitality and helpfulness, joined a family of destiny. At Haran (in modern Syria) she approached a well just as the servant arrived, ready to confront the rather massive job of watering his "ships of the desert," and she offered to help. She also offered lodging to the stranger at her father's house. The servant thanked the Lord and proceeded with his mission, accepting all the offers. He also noted that "the damsel was very fair to look upon, a virgin," and he must have uttered the ancient equivalent of "I came to the right place!"

Most impressed with Rebekah, and with her father Bethuel, the servant "popped the question." Bethuel had no objections and left the decision to Rebekah, who turned out to be as adven-

turesome as she was comely. She agreed to make the trip back to
Canaan with the visitor and to marry his master.

And that is the way they did things back then.

The servant's saddlebags were opened then and Rebekah was
decked out in magnificent jewels and presented with gifts from
her future husband. She was packed in a moment and the two set
out.

It was something of a chancy situation, of course, but Isaac was
immediately delighted with his "blind date" bride. He came forth
from his tent upon the arrival of Rebekah and it was love at first
sight. The two were married in true nomadic fashion, with Abraham officiating in the fields of Hebron.

The young couple stayed on with Abraham for some thirty-five
years until the death of the patriarch. Abraham did not, after all,
live to see much of his valued covenant fulfilled—when he died he
still did not possess the land of Canaan; just a few wells. But he had
seen his son married to a godly Semitic woman, and he enjoyed
the company of rare grandchildren—the twins Jacob and Esau.
Those two, who were already in contention in their mother's
womb, according to the record, must have greatly amused the Father of Many Nations in his last years. Of Abraham it could aptly
be said, "He'd seen it all."

Isaac buried his father on the only land that he truly owned—
the cemetery where Sarah lay at Hebron.

ISAAC THE WELL-DIGGER

Isaac was a most Godly man, believing strongly in the Lord and
in the spiritual inheritance he had received. He was his father's
son, in faith and in his nomadic ways.

Like Abraham, Isaac seemed to prefer the mountains and pastures of Canaan, the land he owned by divine decree. He made no
attempt to capture territory or contest his rights with the pagans
around him, but he did plan ahead in one important way; he dug
wells.

It doesn't sound like much, but the owner of a well in ancient
Canaan was in a very advantageous position. A good well often

meant the difference of feast or famine, life or death. Healthy flocks followed the shepherd who had water; the arid climate of the Holy Land, indifferent to man or beast, killed out the rest.

Digging a well was tantamount to staking out a claim in Canaan. The territory surrounding any well was reckoned to belong to the digger and to his heirs, and this economy was respected by the nomadic sojourners. Practical and patient, Isaac dug many wells.

The new possessor of history's greatest expectations must have been looking ahead to better times for his progeny. Isaac seemed to lead an orderly and peaceful life with his loving wife. Managing the upbringing of the quarrelsome Jacob and Esau may have used up a great deal of his energies.

Little is said about the later life of the nearly sacrificed one. The Scriptures move quickly to the volatile career of one of the Bible's truly fascinating characters, Jacob.

THE HEEL-GRABBER

Jacob's name means "replacer," or "supplanter," and indeed this younger of Rebekah's twins was born clutching his brother's heel.

Rebekah had gone complaining to the Lord about the antagonism within her during her pregnancy—the twins actually were wrestling in her belly, according to the record. God replied interestingly, "Two nations are in thy womb . . . and the elder shall serve the younger" (Gen. 25:23).

The hirsute Esau (whose name means "hairy") and his overcoming brother were finally delivered, to their mother's relief, but the strife between them was to go on for nearly a lifetime. They turned out to be quite different personalities—the subtle Jacob content to mind his tents and conduct intrigues to gain Esau's birthright; and the outdoorsman Esau who loved to hunt and present to his appreciative father delicious venison for special feasts.

Jacob obtained the birthright quite cheaply as things turned out. It seemed that Esau returned from a hunt very hungry one day when he spied Jacob cooking lentils over an open fire. The older brother asked to be fed and Jacob said he would be glad to serve him—for the birthright. Then and there Esau traded away his elder son's right to the covenant of God for one meal.

Esau had never taken his spiritual legacy seriously; God's promises were "pie in the sky" to the earthy he-man. Lentils you could eat; covenants were part of his grandfather's storytelling (Gen. 25:31–34). Esau was easy to bargain with.

The matter came to a head later on when Isaac, now blind and feeble, sought to bless his elder son. He felt he was very near death and he asked that Esau bring his marvelous venison for one last great meal, at which Esau would receive the valuable blessing.

But Jacob came instead, in a peculiar disguise. Plotting with his mother, Jacob conspired to bring some lamb she had prepared, rather in the style of Esau's memorable stews, and he wore a furry animal skin so that Isaac, by touch, would think him to be Esau.

The plots and counterplots within this peculiar family make for some good reading (Gen. 27) but the outcome of it all has Isaac blessing his *younger* son and Esau becoming murderously furious.

At this point Jacob left home, on his mother's advice, and went to Haran where her brother Laban's family resided. Rebekah told Isaac that it would be best for Jacob to seek a wife now, though she privately knew that what was best was to put some distance between Jacob and the deadly huntsman Esau.

Utilizing his father's theory of wife-seeking, Jacob agreed to visit the Semitic tribes of the north. Isaac saw him off with a repetition of the Abrahamic covenant, and God confirmed this in a wonderful dream Jacob enjoyed during the journey (Gen. 28:13–15). Jacob was now the full recipient of God's agreements with Abraham and had no one to fear in all Canaan except his twin brother.

THE BARTERED BRIDES

Jacob met his match as a deceiver in his uncle Laban of Haran.

Laban had two daughters, one plain and one pretty, and Jacob fell in love with Rachel, the younger and prettier, as soon as he arrived. He agreed with Laban to work seven years in his fields for the privilege of marrying Rachel.

Everything was satisfactory until the morning after the wedding. The veiled bride whom Laban had sent into Jacob's darkened marriage tent was not Rachel after all, but Leah, the ugly one. The excited bridegroom was completely fooled.

It was poetic justice and Jacob well knew it, but he certainly voiced his complaint to Laban. Well, his uncle shrugged, it really wasn't the custom in these parts to marry off the younger daughter first, but if Jacob would simply put in another seven years in the field he was welcome to Rachel as well.

It's a wonder that Jacob didn't take Laban behind the tent and kill him, but he agreed to the offer. This time, however, Jacob demanded delivery in advance, and he wed Rachel the following week.

This began a child-bearing competition between the sisters, who vied over which could present Jacob with more sons. These sons, it might be said, stood to inherit the covenant, and this was understood within Jacob's multiple family.

The underrated Leah won the contest hands down. God had a lot to do with that: "When the Lord saw that Leah was hated, he opened her womb: but Rachel was barren" (Gen. 29:31). The following verses celebrate Leah's heroic fertility, as her sons, bearing the names of the tribes of Israel, readily come forth.

The frustrated Rachel then gave her maid, Bilhah, to her husband in the old family tradition, and Bilhah came through with two sons who were more or less credited to Rachel. Not to be undone, Leah presented *her* maid, Zilpah, to the virile Jacob and two more sons came forth.

Then, remarkably, Rachel bore a son of her own. Joseph, a key personality of the Old Testament, and the favorite son of Jacob, was born of Rachel, eleventh in line.

Leah added a daughter somewhere along the way and by the time Jacob's Mesopotamian career ended he had twelve children, two wives, two concubines, and a very impressed uncle Laban. Jacob then planned to return to Canaan, his real home.

He met with Laban and the two sharp traders decided to divide their flocks so that Jacob could take animals with him. The method was to separate the spotted cattle and sheep from the solid-colored ones; the spotted offspring would belong to Jacob and the solid to Laban. Jacob sneakily tried to influence the breeding of the animals by placing striped logs in the fields before their eyes, which had a doubtful effect. Over the next six years, however, Jacob's share of the flocks multiplied impressively, by the Lord's intervention, and the relationship with Laban went sour. The time had come to depart.

The four-hundred-mile trek to Canaan of Jacob's large entourage, including his prodigious family, servants and flocks, was problematical, of course, but Jacob expected a welcome back home. Surely after twenty years Esau would be willing to let bygones be bygones. Esau had settled in Edom and Jacob sent messengers there to tell his brother that he was returning in peace. He extended the hand of fraternal friendship and awaited a reply.

Esau replied that he was waiting to receive Isaac indeed, and in fact he would be glad to come out and welcome him—with four hundred armed men!

Jacob turned to God in prayer. Had not the Almighty advised him to return to Canaan, after all? What was to be the plan, since Esau had such a good memory? Jacob asked God for protection.

Next he devised a strategy for meeting Esau. He sent some servants out with animals as gifts for his brother to mollify him.

He also sent his wives and children forth, apparently feeling that Esau might shrink from killing the patriarch of so large a family of blood relatives. Then Jacob was alone, left to wrestle with his new problem.

COMING TO GRIPS WITH GOD

And wrestle he did—with God!

In one of the strangest episodes in all Scripture, the record now tells of a wrestling match between Jacob and Almighty God. The Person of the Godhead who would most likely be visiting the earth at this point in Scripture has been taken to be Jesus, but in any case it becomes clear as the curious match progresses that Jacob is fighting with the Lord in some form.

Jacob fought well. The match came down to substantially a

draw, though the mortal one's thigh was thrown out of joint. Refusing to capitulate even after this painful injury, Jacob begged God for a blessing. The Lord responded resoundingly: "Thy name shall be called no more Jacob, but Israel: for as a prince hast thou power with God and with men, and hast prevailed" (Gen. 32:28; Israel means "A prince with God").

Some have interpreted this strange event as exemplifying God's direct intervention, in an unmistakable way, in the affairs of Jacob. Perhaps God felt that the faith of the chosen line had deteriorated through the generations, and, truth to tell, Jacob was hardly representative of the overall righteousness of his illustrious grandfather Abraham. God Himself literally "handled" Jacob, leaving him with a permanent injury which required him to limp with a cane for the rest of his life, but the Almighty did not slay him. Undoubtedly Jacob now had a clearer idea of the strength and the mercy of the God of his fathers, and he went forth with new confidence to face Canaan and Esau.

His change of name, of course, has had a permanent effect on history, and the chosen people were henceforth and are still today referred to by the collective term Israel.

Esau, meanwhile, seemed to become choked up at the sight of his many nephews, his niece, and his sisters-in-law. He accepted Jacob's gifts and the brothers were reconciled. Jacob was now to live in Canaan in peace.

The Jewish people later instituted a law in honor of Jacob and his peculiar encounter with the Lord. To this day the Jews do not eat the hindquarter of any meat, in deference to Father Jacob's disability from his wrestling match with God.

As if to celebrate the return to the Promised Land, God blessed Jacob and Rachel with one more son, Benjamin. The joy of the very aged and infirm Isaac at this one last arrival of a grandchild must have been complete, but unfortunately Rachel died in childbirth. She was buried in that small Judean town which has ever been associated with the travail of childbirth, Bethlehem.

But now Jacob had his twelve sons, who became the patriarchal founders of the twelve tribes of Israel. Their names still appear on the façades of synagogues the world around, and we are to hear much more throughout the Old Testament—and the New Testament as well—of the fortunes of the descendants of Jacob's twelve sons. Their imperishable names: Reuben, Simeon, Levi, Judah, Issachar, Zebulun (all by Leah); Gad, Asher (by Zilpah the maid); Dan, Naphtali (by Bilhah the maid); Joseph, Benjamin (by Rachel). Leah's daughter, Dinah, did not found a tribe.

Isaac, his family reassembled, continued to survive, dying finally at the ripe old age of 180. He was buried with his parents at Hebron. Abraham's purchase was still recognized by the descendants of the original sellers of the burial plot, though Hebron is in vital contention today by further descendants who have failed to honor the purchase.

Jacob and his family remained in Canaan for a generation, but in time they departed, this time for an anguishing four-hundred-year stay in the land of Egypt.

4

The Wandering Jews:
Moses and the Exodus

Four hundred years is a very long time for a nation to be enslaved.

We tend not to make accurate comparisons with modern times when we look back a great distance in history. But four centuries —twice the age of the United States—is a very long time for one nation to serve another.

How did the descendants of Abraham find themselves in such a predicament? The matter had been prophesied by the Lord, to be sure, but how did it come about?

"BEHOLD, I HAVE DREAMED A DREAM"

Sibling rivalry was nothing new in the families of the patriarchs of Israel, but it ran dangerously deep among the twelve sons of Jacob. Joseph, Rachel's first son and his father's favorite, was the victim this time. Through God's Will and the marvelous talents of the very gifted Joseph, Egypt now enters the Biblical record again, to the chagrin of the envious eleven.

It seemed that Joseph was able to interpret dreams, and he tended to dream some very untactful dreams which he related to his family. His brothers had begun to look askance at Joseph when his father presented him with the provoking coat of many colors; his tedious dream analyses were the last straw.

Joseph dreamt that his brothers' wheat sheaves bowed down to his own wheat sheaves, and that the sun, moon, and eleven stars bowed down before him. The family did not fail to see the implications of this unsubtle latter dream, and even the partisan Jacob was indignant: "Shall I and thy mother and thy brethren indeed come to bow down ourselves to thee to the earth?" demanded the offended father (Gen. 37:10–11).

The older boys eventually decided that if Joseph were to perish in an unfortunate accident they could all muddle through without further information from the dreamer. One day when Jacob sent Joseph out to the fields to check on his brothers at their flocks (without Benjamin, too young to shepherd as yet) they decided to kill him.

Along came the favorite, resplendent in his gorgeous coat, walking into the trap. The brothers grabbed him and threw him into a ditch while they made their plan. Just then a spice caravan, headed south toward Egypt, happened by; they turned out to be cousins, Ishmaelites. The Arabs, like the Jews, were at their trading businesses four thousand years ago as they are today—spices in one millennium, oil in another; the Middle East doesn't change.

Judah had a brainstorm. They could simply sell Joseph to the caravan as a slave. They would surely never see him again and, besides, they could make some money on the deal. It was done, and the brothers retained that one-of-a-kind coat to show to Jacob. They dipped the coat in sheep's blood and allowed their father to conclude that Joseph had been attacked by a wild beast in the fields.

Poor Jacob mourned his favorite for many years.

JOSEPH THE ECOLOGIST

That was hardly the end of Joseph, however, who was to rise to high places in the Egyptian government.

When the caravan had delivered him he became a steward of Potiphar, the captain of Pharaoh's palace guard, in the Egyptian capital. Unfortunately his employer's wife took a liking to the sensitive young Hebrew and tried to seduce him. When Joseph resisted the advances he found himself accused of rape and jailed.

He remained incarcerated for several years until he happened to draw some important cellmates. Two of Pharaoh's domestics, caught in some court intrigue, were placed in irons with Joseph.

Pharaoh's baker and his butler were the characters and, like any-one else, they dreamt mysterious dreams. Joseph, having little to do with his time, perceptively interpreted for them.

There was good news and bad news; the butler would survive and the baker would be executed. As things turned out Joseph was quite right; in three days the butler was reemployed and the baker hanged.

Some two years passed and the matter seemed forgotten. But then Pharaoh himself had a troubling dream which he was unable to understand. He called in wise men and magicians of the court, to no avail. The butler's memory was jogged (he was alive, after all) and he told Pharaoh about the remarkable Hebrew who lay wasting in his cell. He reviewed for the King the accuracy of Joseph's interpretations (Gen. 41).

Fascinated, Pharaoh called for the Israelite prisoner, who, the record tells us, "shaved himself and changed his raiment," and hustled off to the royal palace.

Pharaoh interviewed Joseph cautiously. "I have dreamed a dream, and there is none that can interpret it: and I have heard say of thee, that thou canst understand a dream to interpret it."

"It is not in me," Joseph answered respectfully. "God shall give Pharaoh an answer of peace."

Pharaoh then gave the specifics of his dream and Joseph inter-preted. There would be seven years of bumper crops for Egypt, Joseph said, followed by seven years of devastating drought and famine. The King ought immediately to begin building a grain reserve during the good years so that there would be enough to withstand the famine.

It would understate to say that Pharaoh was impressed. "Can we find such a one as this is, a man in whom the Spirit of God is?" he exclaimed. And he must have taken Joseph's breath away as he went on, "Forasmuch as God hath shewed thee all this, there is none so discreet and wise as thou art. Thou shalt be over my house, and according unto thy word shall all my people be ruled: only in the throne will I be greater than thou" (Gen. 41:38–40).

Joseph was made second in command over all Egypt because of his dream interpretation! Practically speaking, it was necessary in Pharaoh's mind for Joseph, the one who had the clairvoyant knowledge, to administer the ecological program by which Egypt would survive the coming famine. And, too, Joseph would need extraordinary powers of taxation in order to get the people to give up half their grain each year.

But the move Pharaoh made was still most unusual. First, the Egyptians simply did not like the Hebrew people (Gen. 43:32), a fact as apparent in the days of the Pharaohs as it is now. Second, Joseph had not the vaguest experience with governing, let alone governing Egyptians. Actually the rationale behind Pharaoh's decision was spiritual, as his language indicates. He seemed to recognize and appreciate that God's hand was on Joseph, and this Pharaoh had a reverence for God. His heirs were to treat the Hebrews with considerably less respect, and eventually to pay the price.

God saw fit to bless Egypt in those times. Had he not covenanted with Abraham, "I will bless them that bless thee"? Pharaoh had made an excellent choice.

Joseph's predictions came out to the letter, and God had indeed given Pharaoh an answer of peace. The seven years of famine, which struck the entire Middle East, were no problem for the prepared Egyptians. (Had Joseph been wrong in his dream interpretation, the grain collector would surely have gone the way of the late baker, but of course it was the Lord who guided Rachel's child, as always. Prayerful, and ever mindful of his spiritual legacy, Joseph was a believer who expected and received miracles.)

HIS BROTHERS' KEEPER

The famine hit hard in Canaan, especially among the herdsmen. Barren fields yielded nothing for starving animals, and the nomads wandered without hope.

Jacob's family (or the Israelites, as we may now properly call them) heard of the plenty in Egypt and the ten eldest brothers were dispatched to plead for grain with Pharaoh. Jacob may have supposed that ten members of one starving family would move the Egyptians to pity.

The irony is overwhelming. The Hebrew delegation was assigned to Joseph, the vice-Pharaoh, to whom they might make their appeals. The brothers were now to bow down before the detested Joseph who had dreamt all this so many years before.

They didn't even recognize the splendidly attired sovereign who graced the court of Egypt. If they had been envious of Joseph's simple Canaanite shepherd's coat, what did they think now?

In one of the most moving stories of the entire Bible (Gen. 42–45) Joseph, nearly overcome but always controlling himself, interviews his faithless brothers before his throne.

"You are spies," he accuses them, coldly speaking Egyptian through an interpreter. He demands the youngest among them as a hostage, and so Simeon is given up; the others are to return to their father and bring back Benjamin, whom Jacob had kept at home. So grieved was Jacob still over the loss of Joseph that he could not allow Benjamin to go to Egypt with the others. (Perhaps Joseph feared for the well-being of Benjamin in view of his own former experience with his brothers.)

Pretending to test the validity of their story (but really wanting to see his full brother most of all) Joseph sent them off, secretly filling their bags with money. Actually weeping covertly during the interview, he ordered them back to Canaan.

There Jacob was overcome with the news. He had lost another son and the heartless Egyptians still wanted more. Touchingly he cries before them, "Me have ye bereaved of my children: Joseph is not, and Simeon is not, and ye will take Benjamin away!"

Reuben, the eldest, steps forward with the solemn vow, "Slay my two sons, if I bring him not to thee: deliver him into my hand, and I will bring him to thee again" (Gen. 42:37).

And so the return trip is made with Benjamin along, Jacob's last words ringing in the ears of the distraught Reuben, "If mischief befall him . . . then shall ye bring down my gray hairs with sorrow to the grave."

The brothers now present themselves again before the unfeeling vice-Pharaoh, this time introducing Benjamin as corroboration of their story.

"Is this your younger brother, of whom ye spake unto me?" Joseph inquires indifferently. But then he quickly excused himself and retired to his chambers, totally shattered at the sight of his mother's other son. The record goes on, "And he washed his face, and went out, and refrained himself, and said, set on bread." And the brothers were treated to a palace dinner by their ever more eccentric host.

Now the brothers were supplied with the grain they had sought and sent on their way, but this time Joseph had one of his servants secrete a silver cup from the palace in Benjamin's knapsack. Joseph let them get a short distance out of town and then sent his police to recover the cup and the "thief."

The brothers were taken back to the palace, crestfallen and ashamed. Their host now demanded to keep Benjamin as his servant; the others could go. But how could they go? What would they say to Jacob? They try hopelessly to explain it all to Joseph.

Judah steps forward and fearfully addresses the monarch in petition for the life of Benjamin. He volunteers himself in place of Benjamin, and tearfully concludes, "For how shall I go up to my father, and the lad be not with me?"

At that Joseph finally breaks down and the masquerade is over. But the brothers cannot follow what happens next. Joseph orders the room cleared except for him and his guests, and then stands sobbing uncontrollably before them. Finally he cries in Hebrew, "I am Joseph; doth my father yet live?"

They simply do not comprehend. We can imagine the brothers standing deferentially before the vice-Pharaoh of all Egypt, who has seemed to go mad before their eyes, and they are unable to put this amazing character together with the adolescent boy they sold into slavery in the distant past.

When they finally get the picture quite a reconciliation comes about, with many apologies, as we can imagine. The brothers are still afraid of the powerful Joseph but he gives them quite a lesson in spiritual matters (Gen. 45:7–9), disclosing that all of this is God's plan. He then sends them, laden with goods and treasures —especially Benjamin—back to Canaan. They are to tell their father what had become of his favorite son. They are to return with Jacob and their families to live in Egypt.

If the brothers had trouble assimilating the new situation of Joseph, their father was nearly slain by the news! They didn't put it to him very gently, but simply reported, "Joseph is yet alive, and he is governor over all the land of Egypt."

"And Jacob's heart fainted, for he believed them not," the Scriptures relate. But when Jacob saw the fine wagons Joseph had sent along he recovered himself. He stated simply, "It is enough; Joseph my son is yet alive: I will go and see him before I die" (Gen. 45:28).

TO THE LAND O' GOSHEN

People speak of "the land o' Goshen" as some far-off place at the end of the earth, and in a way it was, to the Canaanite Jacob. It was in the Egyptian province of Goshen that the Hebrew family was to settle, a rich Nile-delta pastureland ideal for their husbandry, but of course Jacob realized that he was leaving the Promised Land.

Nevertheless, God confirmed that this was a good move, in an appearance to Jacob, and so the large family—sons, wives, children, and 147-year-old patriarch—left the famished Canaan. God reassured Jacob that the Hebrews would yet be "a great nation."

Back in Egypt, Pharaoh also confirmed that the family of his valued assistant were indeed welcome. It was under no special duress, then, that the Jewish people went down into Egypt. Later developments under less accommodating Pharaohs would cause Moses to cry in the Egyptian court, "Let my people go!" but for the present the seventy Israelites were more than satisfied with the graciousness of Egypt.

Having seen his beloved Joseph at last, Jacob died in peace, but not before uttering a magnificent series of blessings upon his twelve sons—blessings containing stunningly accurate prophecies (Gen. 49). Included among the pronouncements of Jacob was the important prediction that the Tribe of Judah would be the royal line of Israel. Indeed, the mighty Kings David and Solomon and their descendants did in fact rule Israel later on, and Jesus, "The King of the Jews," was also of the Tribe of Judah.

Jacob's dying request was that his body be taken back to Hebron and laid with his forebears Abraham and Isaac. This was done, and we can imagine the emotional funeral of Jacob, the last of the three patriarchs of Israel, as his family laid him to rest in the burial ground still respected by the honest herdsmen of Canaan as belonging to the Hebrews.

Life went along peacefully for the sons of Jacob in Egypt. They were certainly not as yet enslaved, and they prospered with Pharaoh's blessings. The seven years of bad crops came and went as Joseph had predicted.

At Joseph's death there was further prophecy. The loyal servant of Egypt, he had never forgotten that he was an Israelite and that God had promised a great destiny to his people. He was content to be buried in Egypt, but he asked that when God would deliver the Hebrews back to Canaan his body be exhumed and reburied at Hebron. He reassured the family at his death that God would surely take their descendants back out of Egypt and continue with his plan to make them a great nation.

THE FINAL SOLUTION

Hitler was hardly the first to try to find "the final solution" to what has been regarded through the ages by anti-Semites as "the Jewish problem." The Egyptians once tried an unthinkably cruel method for controlling the Jewish numbers in their nation. They stooped to infanticide—the killing of babies.

The Jewish problem on that occasion had grown slowly out of the inherent distaste of Egyptians for Hebrews. After Joseph's time things deteriorated rapidly for the Israelites in Egypt, until they became slaves to the native population. Under the whip, the Israelites built great Egyptian monuments, the stone fortresses Pithom and Raamses, which held the national treasury of the land. The Egyptians had long forgotten the life-saving mission of Joseph, and the Israelites were just another oppressed minority over the following four centuries.

The Jews prayed constantly for a deliverer, aware of God's promises and always seeking their fulfillment. They dreamed of a powerful leader who might stand up to Pharaoh and put an end to this injustice.

The Hebrews multiplied rapidly in Egypt, so that the original seventy were to become two million by the end of the prophesied period of slavery. Their prolific growth did not go unnoticed in the royal palace, and Pharaoh was informed by his political advisors that the Hebrews could become a dangerous fifth column in the nation if something weren't done about their birthrate.

The suggestion of infanticide was designed not only to limit the Hebrew population, but also to circumvent the possibility of this prayed-for deliverer actually coming forward. It was decided that all of the male babies would be killed at birth. This would not affect the present slave population, of course, and it was a system that could be varied as the times required. Perhaps later on a few more Jewish males could be spared to breed future slaves, and in the meanwhile the population would surely decrease drastically.

Little did Pharaoh realize that his odious scheme would backfire in a most ironic way. The deliverer was born, to be sure, and ultimately raised and educated in the household of Pharaoh himself!

OUT OF THE BULRUSHES

Though we have looked at the lives of faithful men thus far: Abel the righteous; Noah, who alone was spared; Abraham, the patient one; Lot of Sodom; Isaac and Jacob, who clung to the Promised Land and refused to marry pagans; Joseph the mighty; we have not yet seen the equal of Moses.

He is incomparably the deliverer of his people, the emancipator of two million slaves, the overwhelmer of Pharaoh. Personally, he led an entire nation to liberty.

In speaking of the ministry of his own Son, God calls Jesus Christ "a prophet like unto Moses" (Deut. 18:15). Moses enjoyed more momentous interviews with God Almighty than any man before or after him. He presented the nation of Israel, and the world, the Law of God. He authored the Pentateuch under the inspiration of the Lord, and for all we have said thus far we are totally indebted to Moses.

He is the only human being who ever saw God.

He was spared a very early death when his desperate mother put him afloat in a small boat in the Nile. Thousands of Hebrew infants were being slain all around her, and this was the best she could think of. Undoubtedly her son would be killed as well but she would be spared the agony of having him torn from her arms.

Moses, the descendant of Levi, drifted down the river peacefully as his anxious sister followed on the bank. The boat happened to find its way into a private area where the daughter of Pharaoh was bathing and the young lady was immediately taken with the beautiful Hebrew child. Moses' sister boldly approached when she saw Pharaoh's daughter hold the baby, and the sister suggested that she could provide a Hebrew nursing mother for Moses (Moses' own mother of course). The princess, counting it a lucky day, said she would adopt the baby and accept the nursing mother as well.

And so it was, in the providence of God, that the deliverer of the Israelites was to be raised and educated at Pharaoh's expense.

A product of the Egyptian culture, Moses still felt loyalty to his own oppressed people. At the age of forty he tried to come forward as a leader of the Israelites but they wouldn't have him at that point. He became infuriated one day when he saw an Egyptian beating a Hebrew slave and he killed the Egyptian, only to end up with a price on his head. He was obliged to flee into the Sinai desert, to the territory of the Midianites. The former sophisticate of the Egyptian court now took up life as a nomadic herdsman near Mount Sinai.

In a peculiar reverse of the scene at the well in Haran between Abraham's servant and Rachel, Moses encounters his future wife by helping her water *her* animals. He married Zipporah, the daughter of Jethro, a descendant of Ishmael, and lived forty more years in the desert.

Seeking only peace and quiet, the fugitive was visited by great miracles of God. One day while tending his flocks Moses chanced to see a bush burning on Mount Sinai. This was not so unusual a sight, but this bush was never consumed; it burned and burned until Moses finally came closer to inspect it (Ex. 3:3).

As Moses stood by the curious bush the voice of God thundered out at him, "MOSES! MOSES!"

"*Hineni,*" answered the stunned Hebrew, "Here I am." It was an expression of obedience used by his ancestor Abraham in many a conference with God.

God makes quite a speech. He is aware, He says, of the oppression of His chosen people in the land of Egypt; He means to now get them out. We can almost hear Moses asking, "Why tell *me* all this?" but God concludes grandly, "Come now therefore, and I will send thee unto Pharaoh, that thou mayest bring forth the children of Israel out of Egypt!"

Many of us would answer in Moses' very words—"Who am I?"—and it is certain that Moses was not looking forward to seeing Pharaoh, under the circumstances.

"Certainly I will be with thee," God assures the shocked Moses, but the Hebrew seems to stall for time. "Who shall I say sent me?" he stammers to God, in effect.

And God now reveals His name, for the first time in the Bible. "I AM THAT I AM," says God, cryptically, which is given in Hebrew as the unpronounceable "YHWH" (usually said as "Yahweh.")

Moses now continues to object. The Hebrews won't believe him, he says. The Egyptians are powerful. God makes thunderous pronouncements enough to stir a dead man, but the cautious Moses is difficult to move. "And I will stretch out my hand, and smite Egypt with all my wonders!" God declares, as the astonished Moses, hiding his eyes, listens in fear.

God finally demonstrates miracles before Moses, making his shepherd's staff into a snake, and turning his hand leprous and then healthy again. He tells Moses that these wonders will be at his disposal if his people doubt his authority. He will be able to turn river water into blood before their eyes, God tells him.

Amazingly, Moses still objects. Considering the marvelous success of his mission ultimately, Moses is one of the slowest starters in the Scriptures! Now he complains that he is not a particularly good speaker (Ex. 4:10).

God begins to grow impatient and a bit sardonic. "Who hath made man's mouth?" inquires the Creator. "Or who maketh the dumb, or deaf, or the seeing, or the blind? Have not I, the Lord?" Then God declares that if Moses feels he is not eloquent enough for the mission his brother Aaron can do the talking. The two will go and Aaron will be the spokesman for Moses. Moses is to carry that miraculous rod with which he will perform wonders when necessary.

At length Moses accepts the terms and prepares his family for the trip to Egypt. Aaron by his side, and his trusty rod at the ready, he confronts the elders of Israel in their bondage.

They are not so skeptical this time, particularly when Moses shows his remarkable signs from God. They regard that their prayers of centuries are about to be answered "and they bowed their heads and worshipped" (Ex. 4:29–31).

Convincing the Hebrews was one thing; now Moses and Aaron presume to speak with Pharaoh.

GOD VERSUS PHARAOH

Pharaoh was a hard man, perfectly oblivious to the suffering of the legion of slaves in his land. He certainly had no respect for the God of Israel, having plenty of gods of his own, and while he seems to have forgiven and forgotten Moses' earlier crime under the reign of the previous Pharaoh, he is in no way moved by the request for extradition of the Hebrews. Moses and Aaron meet with ironhearted resistance in the Egyptian court.

"Let my people go," cries Moses, "in the Name of the Lord."

"Well, I don't think I know your Lord," retorts Pharaoh, "and I don't care to let your people go. Now, get back to work."

Moses then demonstrates a shocking miracle before Pharaoh, turning his rod into a serpent. Not to be outdone, Pharaoh calls forth the court magicians, and they performed the same trick— throwing their rods to the floor and making them into snakes. Pharaoh thus laughed off the first miracle of Moses, not comprehending that the real battle here was between God and Satan. (Moses' snake devoured those produced by the Egyptians.)

Now, the famous battle of wills continues, as Pharaoh redoubles the duties of the Hebrew slaves, while Moses repeatedly presents threatening miracles before the King. As Moses unveils God's mighty plagues upon Egypt, Pharaoh is hard put to keep pace. The sorcerers of the Egyptian royal house were utterly confounded when the Nile River, an object of worship for all Egyptians, was turned into putrid blood.

And then the plagues fall, one by one, as Pharaoh's heart becomes harder and harder—frogs, flies, lice, diseases of the cattle, total darkness, and on and on. It was now the Egyptian portion of the nation that was suffering under Pharaoh's stubbornness, as the Lord multiplied the woes of the oppressors. The Egyptian miracle makers were far outdistanced by the Almighty. Moses and Aaron were winning their point.

Finally, the dreadful tenth plague hit—the death of the firstborn son in every Egyptian household.

THE PASSOVER PLOT

The night of the exodus from Egypt is, of course, one of the most significant moments in the entire history of Israel, and, in a greater way, in the entire story of religious faith of every Biblical kind. God gave very detailed instructions (Ex. 12) as to the use of unleavened bread, bitter herbs, and most particularly the sacrifice of the lamb. The sacrificial blood, placed on the doorposts, was a sign to the avenging angel to omit the Hebrew households in that horrible night of mass murder in Egypt. The saving blood of the lamb is a symbol intensified throughout the Old Testament, and becomes the prime doctrine of the New Testament. Through the blood, the Hebrews, and New Testament believers as well, receive salvation from slavery.

During that singular night, there was feasting and rejoicing in the Hebrew homes as the Israelites realized that their exodus was at hand. But in the Egyptian homes was death and mourning, and the people would "wail such as not been heard before or since in any other nation." Parents all over Egypt awoke to discover their oldest boy dead.

God did not spare the royal palace. Pharaoh's own son, the very heir to the throne of Egypt, was found dead in his bed. The stricken Pharaoh relented, finally, and now decreed that the Hebrew people could go. Thus, after four hundred long years of bondage, the alien nation of slaves organized into their twelve tribes and debarked in a massive horde toward the Red Sea. Before leaving, they asked the Egyptians for gold, silver, and jewels, and they received them; perhaps the Egyptians, smitten as they were by this insurmountable plague, realized that reparations were due to the Chosen People of God.

For several days, the Israelites marched through the barren Egyptian desert, following a circuitous route—the Lord had commanded them not to take the normal Mediterranean caravan highway, but to head southeast toward the Red Sea coast. Back in the capital, Pharaoh had recovered from his first shock and now reconsidered his decision. Despite the immense wrath of the Lord that had fallen on Egypt in these ten mighty plagues, the single-minded Pharaoh regretted losing his millions of slaves. He quickly assembled a chariot division, and ordered them to chase the Israelites and bring them back, or slaughter them.

Trapped against the Red Sea, the Israelites saw the chariot army swooping down upon them. Unarmed, largely composed of women, children, and old men, the terrified Hebrew nation now faced immediate destruction.

But now, Moses, completely confident of the power of Jehovah, stepped forward with his mighty rod, and as the Lord held back the chariots with a cloud of fire, the deliverer cried, "Stand still and see the salvation of our God!" At that, the Red Sea split— divided into two walls of water, with a dry channel between. Certainly, no man to that time had ever seen the like of this incredible miracle, and perhaps it stands unequaled in the entire Bible.

In any case, the huge Hebrew nation quickly fled through the dry channel, with the Egyptians in hot pursuit. As the chariots tried to negotiate the temporarily dry Red Sea bed, the walls of water cascaded in on them and destroyed the entire army.

There was a vast victory celebration among the Hebrews on the east bank, now. Moses composed a song of victory and tremendous jubilation occurred, as the Hebrews realized that they were free of their oppression at last. It was the faith of the people and the blood of the lamb that delivered God's chosen from Egypt.

Things weren't so simple for the Israelites at this point, of course. Their vast multitude had to be moved through the inhospitable Sinai Desert, and, despite the provisions of God—miraculous sources of water and bread (manna from heaven)—the trip to Mount Sinai was arduous. However, God awaited His people at the Mount where He had first called out Moses, and to the Mount they were to go.

At Mount Sinai, God offers the Law to the children of Israel, and they accept it. The means was for Moses to ask the people their preference on receiving God's commands, and for Moses to report back to the Lord. A subtle change now seems apparent in the record in the relationship between God and Israel. It is almost as if Jehovah is somewhat displeased that the people accept the idea of the Law. Conceivably, they should have replied, "No, we could never obey the divine commands; instead, let us follow the Lord by pure faith and depend only on His mercy." Perhaps Jehovah was disconcerted with the Israelis' willingness to put a sort of business-like, or legal, implication into what formerly had been a love relationship.

The Almighty, who had been so closely involved with His people throughout the exodus, now seems to withdraw up the mountain, with awesome thunder and lightning. It is made clear that if anyone approaches God's position on Mount Sinai, that person will die; only Moses is invited into the now dreadful presence of the Lord.

The problem of the Law is one of theological conjecture. True enough, the Hebrews were never able to properly keep it, the record bears out, but what human beings could? Did the Hebrew nation opt for second-best in God's plans at Sinai? Interestingly, the New Testament is ultimately distinguished from the Old in the fact that it presents no laws, but grants salvation as a free gift in response to faith (Eph. 2:8-9).

In any case, the Israelis had chosen Law, and Law they now got, in good measure. Moses went up to Mount Sinai to receive the voluminous commandments of God.

The Lord gave Moses a legal system divided into three parts: the Moral Law, the Governmental Law, and the Worship Law. Taken together, this massive collection of laws covers nearly four whole books of the Bible, concluding in Deuteronomy, the final book of the Pentateuch. It is fair to say that a great many legal systems of the world today find their roots in the copious anthology of laws given by God on Sinai.

The Moral Law, characterized by the Ten Commandments, established the fundamental relationships between man and God, and between man and man. Moses was given the Ten Commandments on stone tablets, carved by the finger of God. These tablets, depicted today in every synagogue, represent the true Biblical law in its essence.

The Governmental Law, in all its variety, dealt with how the nation of Israel was to be run. It consists of the principles of government, justice for the citizens, numerous statutes dealing with property rights, personal liability, marital disruption, dietary regulations, and a thousand other specifics of daily life. The Governmental Law is extremely detailed, and has been the subject of some thirty-five hundred years of intensive study by Jewish and Gentile scholars.

The Worship Law concerns the rituals of animal sacrifice, the establishment of the Tribe of Levi as the official priesthood, the building of a portable tabernacle, wherein God would dwell and man would be able to worship in His presence. There is also the creation of an annual calendar, with three festival periods designated as holy seasons, when every male Israelite was required to worship God at the tabernacle.

Further details of the Law, which we might look at now, accompanied its initial presentation. The Sabbath was designated as the official sign of the Law covenant between God and Israel, in the manner that circumcision was the sign of the Abrahamic covenant. It was made clear by God that one of the primary purposes of the various laws was to separate Israel from the pagan nations around them. They were to remain consecrated—virtually a different kind of civilization—in order to fulfill God's national purposes for them—the writing of the Bible and the production of the Messiah.

The rabbis say there are 613 laws, in all, varying from the basic ultimatums of the Ten Commandments to incredibly detailed and specific statutes dealing with every imaginable human situation. For a citizen of Israel to merely *know* all the laws was a feat in itself; to keep them, an impossibility.

THE GOLDEN CALF

Remarkably, the Israelites broke the law while it was still being given. Not even waiting for a complete copy of God's statutes and commandments, they did that which was obviously evil in the sight of the Lord; they made an idol.

Moses was being instructed on the Mount for forty days, and the encamped Israelites seemed to grow tired of waiting. Somehow, Aaron went along with the plan to make a calf of gold and worship it, in view of the long silence from Sinai. This astonishing indiscretion, almost unbelievable on the surface of it, may well describe the poverty of the human spiritual condition in any age. Forty days was too long a time to wait for people now apparently spoiled by repeated miracles.

The Lord grew angry on Sinai, understandably, and sent Moses down to discipline the people. The deliverer walked into a scene which dumbfounded him. The chosen people had worked themselves up into a genuine pagan orgy, pouring their allegiance into their ridiculous statue and acting no differently than the Canaanite tribes which their forefathers had abhorred.

In his fury, Moses smashed the tablets of the Ten Commandments and had three thousand people executed at that abominable scene. The invariable penalty for breaking the Law was death.

God was to restore the tablets, and the Israelites were to remember for a long time—though not forever—that idolatry was "an abomination unto the Lord."

While the Jewish law was inflexible—carved in stone, as it were—it had an ongoing component of mercy. Through sacrificial worship, any man could escape the penalty of death by substituting an animal. God's presence remained in the Tabernacle, where the sacrifices were made, and it was indicated by the "Shekinah Glory," a bright light, that hovered over the Tabernacle at all times.

THE ABORTED INVASION

After the Israelites received the Law, they continued journeying toward Canaan to invade it and occupy the Promised Land. Reaching Kadesh-Barnea, in the Negev area, south of Canaan, the elders selected twelve spies to infiltrate the target area and look over its defenses. The reconnaissance mission was also supposed to verify the claims that Canaan was a land "flowing with milk and honey." Naturally, the Israelites were mindful that Canaan was a land of famine when their ancestors chose to leave it.

When the twelve spies returned to the encampment, their reports varied. That the land was bountiful was clear (it took two men to carry one huge bunch of grapes, which they brought as evidence of the fertility of Canaan). But the majority report, by ten of the spies, was that the defenses were impregnable. Great giants protected the land, they stated, and it was hopeless for the Hebrews to invade.

The minority report, given by Caleb and the military genius Joshua, was that the Lord could certainly overcome the defenses of Canaan on behalf of His people.

The difficult matter was put to a vote. The entire nation had come this far, after all, for the express purpose of occupying Canaan. Many a wondrous miracle had accompanied their journey so far, but now they seemed to lose heart. The election returns showed that the majority opinion of the spies had convinced the people at large; Canaan was declared too difficult to attack.

The Almighty was angry with the results of the election, and declared that that particular generation would not enter Canaan, indeed, but would die in the desert after forty years of wandering. It would be left to the following generation to take over the land the Lord had promised, assuming that *they* could muster the necessary faith.

Now the entire Hebrew nation became nomadic wanderers in the desert, and God ministered to their needs despite His discouragement. Through the miraculous production of water from rocks, the manna and great flocks of birds that ordinarily never fly over the desert, the Israelites were fed. Their shoes didn't wear out in forty years of foot travel, according to the record, and God was always present—a pillar of clouds by day, providing shade from the terrible heat, and a pillar of fire by night, providing relief from the numbing coldness of the darkened desert, guided them all the while. Moses remained in command during the entire forty years, reaching the age of one hundred and twenty. We are informed that he did not seem to grow old: "His eye was not dim, nor his natural force abated" (Deut. 34:7).

MOSES' BLUNDER

Moses made what seemed to be a small mistake, but, in principle, one that offended the Almighty. The patriarch became angry with his people for their complaining. It was all right for God to be angry with Israel, but not Moses. He was merely one of the Israelites.

Desert life was very hard, of course, and the people who could not assemble enough faith to enter Canaan now found their wanderings very bitter. On an occasion when Moses was supposed to speak to a rock to produce water, according to the Lord's direction, he gave the rock a smiting in his anger and frustration. Because of that, God said, Moses would never enter the Promised Land.

It seems a shame that one who worshipped and trusted for at least eighty years would not live to see the fruition of all of his prayers, but the Lord was illustrating a principle. God alone is just; God alone is merciful; God alone is angry.

Meanwhile, people died and children were born, and slowly the irreverent generation passed away in the desert, and a new one, more determined than ever to take the Promised Land, was raised up. God guided Moses to commission Joshua finally to lead the Israelites into Canaan, and Moses made a last request of the Lord: Could he but look upon the land? The wandering Jews had now come to the eastern border of Canaan in the Dead Sea area, and Moses was very close, indeed, to his lifetime goal.

The Lord relented and allowed him to climb Mount Nebo, which overlooked the Jordan River Valley. Moses looked across the Jordan and feasted his eyes on Israel. He died on the spot, and the Lord, Himself, buried him there on the mountain.

The forty-year penalty was now passed, and the older generation had died off. A younger, stronger Israelite nation, under the fearless leadership of Joshua, prepared to enter Canaan. It had been a remarkable sojourn; the ups and downs of Israelite faith seem unparalleled in history. First, the entire nation trusted God to get them out of Egypt, and even across the formidable Red Sea. Then they deteriorated into idolatry by the sacred Mount Sinai. Bouncing back from that very negative experience, they had at least intended their invasion at Kadesh-Barnea, but then they lost heart.

How difficult it is for men to believe in God when the chips are down.

But now, with the end of the Pentateuch and a revitalized Israel, the Biblical saga takes a turn for the better.

The Torah, the first five books of the Bible, ends with a heartfelt tribute to the fallen deliverer Moses. "No man knoweth of his sepulchre unto this day," the Book of Deuteronomy concludes, since God Himself had laid His servant to rest.

And the children of Israel wept for Moses in the plains of Moab thirty days: so the days of weeping and mourning for Moses were ended.

And there arose not a prophet since in Israel like unto Moses, whom the Lord knew face to face.

In all the signs and the wonders, which the Lord sent him to do in the land of Egypt to Pharaoh, and to all his servants, and to all his land.

And in all that mighty hand, and in all the great terror which Moses shewed in the sight of all Israel. (Deut. 34:8, 10–12)

5

The Walls Came Tumbling Down: Joshua at Jericho

Joshua was specially commissioned and specially instructed by the Almighty Himself in the conquest of Canaan and the leadership of the Hebrew nation.

> And Joshua the son of Nun was full of the spirit of wisdom; for Moses had laid his hands upon him: and the children of Israel hearkened unto him, and did as the Lord commanded Moses. (Deut. 34:9)

God told Joshua bluntly:

> Moses my servant is dead; now therefore arise, go over this Jordan, thou, and all this people, unto the land which I do give to them, even to the children of Israel.

> Every place that the sole of your foot shall tread upon, that have I given unto you, as I said unto Moses. (Josh. 1:2–3)

And God made very clear that Joshua was not merely to be a soldier, but also a Law-keeping Israelite, of the highest spiritual order:

> Only be thou strong and very courageous, that thou mayest observe to do according to all the law, which Moses my servant commanded thee: turn not from it to the right hand or to the left, that thou mayest prosper whithersoever thou goest.

> This book of the law shall not depart out of thy mouth; but thou shalt meditate therein day and night, that thou mayest observe to do according to all that is written therein: for then

thou shalt make thy way prosperous, and then thou shalt have good success. (Josh. 1:7–8)

THE CONQUEST OF CANAAN

Now, of course, the Promised Land wasn't exactly an empty place waiting to be filled. It was well populated with the numerous idolatrous tribes found there centuries before in the times of the patriarchs. The Lord had said He was waiting for their iniquity to become full—for the Canaanites really to earn the punishment He had in mind for them. And by this time, the paganism in Canaan had surely reached an apex. Archaeology has uncovered the totally depraved society of these early idolaters. Temple prostitution, human sacrifices, and the like were the order of the religions of the Promised Land.

God now told Israel to kill every man, woman, and child in the land; a hard judgment, but, from God's point of view, the removal of a grotesque cancer from a holy place.

Jericho was chosen as the point of initial attack, a green and lush oasis surrounded by the arid hills near the north end of the Dead Sea. It was approachable across the Jordan, in Joshua's estimation. The new leader sent two secret agents into Jericho to inspect the defenses of the city.

The spies are detected. They are hidden in a local harlot's house. Rahab, of questionable reputation but uncommon spiritual grace, tells Joshua's men that she believes God has given Israel the land. (The Canaanites had, of course, heard of the Red Sea disaster that befell Egypt.) Rahab wanted to help the Israelites. She hid the spies from the police, asking them only to spare her and her family when they took the city. She was certain of their ultimate victory. The spies instructed her to hang a red rope out of her window when the attack began. Her house was situated directly on the city wall, and the red rope would be spotted by the first invaders. Then the spies returned to the Hebrew encampment across the Jordan.

Meanwhile, the twelve tribes were beginning to cross the river— no small problem. The invasion was planned during the spring floods, and the Jordan was about a half mile wide; but, just as Moses had his Red Sea miracle, Joshua conquered the Jordan. The upstream waters were stopped at the command of the Israelite general, while the downstream waters kept on rolling, creating a clear, dry path across the riverbed. The Levitical priests led the way, carrying the Ark of the Covenant, in which was kept the tablets of the Ten Commandments, Aaron's rod, and manna from the desert. As soon as their feet touched the water, it rolled back.

The defenders of Jericho were completely surprised at this unlikely attack from the river side of the city; but if that particular onslaught impressed them, they must really have been astonished at what happened next. The Hebrews, following God's instructions to the letter, brought no battering rams, no ladders, no flying stones, spears, or arrows. The Lord had told Joshua that Israel should march around the city one time each day, for six days, with seven priests marching in front of the Ark, blowing ram's horns. On the seventh day, they marched around seven times, and when the seven priests blew the seven trumpets the seventh time, Joshua gave the command to attack.

The attack seemed more noisy than dangerous to the defenders, no doubt, but the walls of Jericho, certified to be eleven feet thick by archaeologists, were no match for the clamor:

So the people shouted when the priests blew with the trumpets: and it came to pass, when the people heard the sound of the trumpet, and the people shouted with a great shout, that the wall fell down flat, so that the people went up into the city, every man straight before him, and they took the city. (Josh. 6:20)

This story leaves most Bible readers speechless, but the brilliant commentator C. I. Scofield said: "The central truth here is that spiritual victories are won by means and upon principles utterly foolish and inadequate in the view of human wisdom." Rahab's house was spared, and she and her family survived the attack though the Israelites went about the letter of God's command concerning the rest of Jericho. The population was annihilated by the Israeli army.

DEFEAT AT AI

A confident Israeli regiment was then dispatched to the little nearby village of Ai, after the heady victory at Jericho. But, somehow, the Israelite fortunes reversed. Ai successfully defended itself, and there were many invader casualties. The Hebrew army fell back and Joshua made entreaties to God. Surely, the Almighty, who had parted the Jordan and thrown down the walls of mighty Jericho, did not intend to stop the conquest at the unimportant town of Ai.

Joshua had gone to the right source for his answer. God now revealed that Israel had sinned (Josh. 7:11-12). All the spoils of Jericho were to go into the treasury of the Lord, but someone among the Hebrews had stolen some of the property for himself, and the Lord had withdrawn his protective shield from his people.

Joshua quickly found the culprit, Achan of the Tribe of Judah, and a court-martial was organized. Achan confessed to misappropriating some expensive Babylonian clothing, fifty pieces of silver, and a large chunk of gold (Josh. 7:21). He was remorseful, realizing that his greed had caused the defeat of the Hebrew army. But in keeping with the uncompromising law of Sinai, Achan and his family were taken out of their tent and stoned to death by the people. Now the army could proceed with the conquest, with God's blessings.

They began again at Ai, this time rolling over the town with no difficulty.

THE NEGEV AND CENTRAL CANAAN

With the frontier city of Jericho out of the way, Canaan was mortally weakened. The whole country now lay exposed to the Hebrew invasion. Joshua's strategy was to take the southern and central areas before heading into mountainous Samaria and the north.

The stubborn Canaanites largely stood their ground, though the stories of the miracle-working Hebrew army were now well known, and the Israelites had gained a fearsome reputation for taking no prisoners. The Scriptures say that the Lord put it in the hearts of the Canaanites to challenge Israel and battle all up and down the country.

Five city Kings, led by the King of Jerusalem, organized for a counterattack, but were wiped out in one miraculous blow. This was the day when the sun stood still (Josh. 10:12–14). "And there was no day like that before it or after it," the record tells us, believably enough.

Southern and central opposition was soon overcome, as Joshua paused for a mopping-up operation.

Many Canaanite tribes had now been eliminated, but the Gibeonites, who had thus far not joined in the opposition, made a shrewd move. They well understood that Israel was unbeatable. They alone, among the Holy Land occupiers, seemed to appreciate the hopelessness of confronting the inspired armies of the Hebrews. Loath to surrender, under the circumstances, they devised a plan to kid the Israelites into thinking that they were not Canaanites at all. They sent a delegation out to meet the Hebrews, and the men wore a peculiar disguise. They dressed in worn-out clothing and shoes, with dirt all over them, looking as though they had been traveling many months. They related to Joshua that they had come a great distance, from outside of Canaan, and wished to align themselves with Israel and do the menial work, such as drawing water and cutting wood.

Joshua omitted consulting the Lord about this seemingly minor matter (Josh. 9:14), and accepted the Gibeonites as a magnanimous gesture. Israel lived to regret that decision for centuries. Joshua soon discovered the ruse, of course, but he had given his word, and he honored it. The Gibeonites later located in the central highlands of the country, and were a constant thorn to Israel —later contributing to the division of the nation.

GALILEE AND THE NORTH

Holding the southern area securely, Joshua now marched his armies against Galilee and the more distant northern territories. The story was the same all over again; no one could confront the Israelite forces successfully. By the time the conquest ended, the Hebrews had occupied almost all of the designated divine land grant, from the Wadi of Egypt north past the Sea of Galilee and Mount Hermon, nearly to the Euphrates.

There were pockets of Canaanites left in the land, however, and for some reason Joshua didn't pursue them to the last community. They would live to cause quite a bit of trouble for Israel in the future, but the Hebrews had decided they had conquered enough land and had enough war for a while.

It was time now to divide the land and give each of the twelve tribes its portion. Joshua was called upon to divide the land more or less laterally, west to east, from the Mediterranean Sea to the Jordan River Valley. Each sector was about the size of an average American county. Once the land divisions were surveyed, the various tribes drew lots for each piece. Judah drew the portion that included the City of Jerusalem. Levi, being the priestly tribe, did not have a land inheritance (Deut. 10:8–9), but was given certain cities throughout the country. The half tribes of Manasseh and Ephraim (sons of Joseph) were each given portions. Also, two other tribes had already staked out their inheritance on the east side of the Jordan before Moses' death.

The body of Joseph, brought out of Egypt according to his last wishes, and carried throughout the entire forty years in the wilderness and the conquest of Canaan, was now buried in the Promised Land. Joseph was interred at Shechem, in the sector of Manasseh.

HERE COME THE JUDGES

Now a peculiar form of government was set up in Israel. There was no central capital, although Shiloh, where the Tabernacle was set up, was the recognized center of religious worship.

The country could be called a "theocracy," where God rules His people directly, but it was also often in anarchy. The expression "everybody did their own thing" is not so contemporary, after all. Judg. 21:25 informs us "every man did that which was right in his own eyes."

Idolatry began to creep into the worship of the Hebrews. Periods of godly peace varied with departures from the Lord, which invariably seemed to result in military oppression from the remaining Canaanites. The neighboring Moabites and Mesopotamians were also forces to be reckoned with in those days.

But, in truth, what Abraham, Isaac, Jacob, Joseph, and Moses had longed for was now a reality. Israel was a bona fide nation of the world, by approximately 1400 B.C.

The new nation had its ups and downs for a few centuries. It seemed that when the people would return to the Lord for deliverance, He would raise up a Judge (as much a military leader as a judicial one). The Judge would deliver the people and restore peace. But, all in all, there was a constant spiritual and military roller coaster in the Promised Land. Rebellion, judgment, repentance, and restoration revolved in turn for some four hundred years, as twelve men and one woman from the various tribes served as Judges of Israel. Some of the most fascinating stories of the Bible appear in this little-read section concerning the reign of the Judges.

Take Ehud, the Left-Handed Assassin. Israel was suffering oppression from powerful Moab, on the east side of the Dead Sea, and King Eglon was collecting tribute. In answer to prayer, the Lord raised up the powerful left-handed Ehud from the Tribe of Benjamin. The new Judge went with a delegation to bring periodic taxes from the Israelites to King Eglon.

On the return trip, Ehud seemed to get an inspiration and told his men he had a confidential message for the King and would have to return to the palace. King Eglon, observing no sword on the left thigh of the returnee, cleared his throne room to hear the secret message. As Ehud approached the King, he pulled his dagger from his right hip with his left hand, and stabbed Eglon through the abdomen. Eglon was so fat, the record tells us, that the entire dagger was covered up. Ehud locked the throne room doors on his way out, and the palace guard did not disturb the

King, who they imagined was in his bathroom, as the record relates. Once back in Israel, Ehud organized an army and overthrew the leaderless Moabites. Thus the Lord delivered Israel, in this instance, and they had peace for eighty years.

Deborah was a liberated woman of over three thousand years ago, who was a Judge of Israel and also a prophetess. She ruled over a situation where the north had fallen into rebellion and idolatry, so that the Canaanite King Jabin controlled northern Israel out of his capital in Hazor (in northern Galilee). Jabin depended on a vicious and capable general named Sisera, who terrorized the area with nine hundred iron chariots.

Deborah told the tribe of Zebulun's military leader, Barak, to gather ten thousand foot soldiers at Mount Tabor, and she prophesied that he would defeat Sisera's cavalry in the Valley of Jezreel. Barak agreed, but only if Deborah would personally accompany the army. The prophetess consented, but uttered the interesting fact that a woman would kill Sisera, instead of Barak having that honor.

When the battle began, Barak's infantry attacked the chariots. They would have been cut to pieces by the horses and the huge wheels, but the Lord sent a tremendous rain storm, making the Kishon River overflow in a flash flood. The heavy chariots now bogged down in the mud and the Canaanites, stripped of their advantage, were soundly defeated by the Israelites (Judg. 4:14–15; 5:20–22).

General Sisera, hardly one to go down with the ship, escaped on foot and ran off to a little nomadic settlement, where he met the accommodating Jael, a descendant of Moses' father-in-law, Jethro. She invited him to stay in her tent, and while he slept, she pounded a ten-inch nail through his skull, temple to temple.

With Sisera out of the way, Barak's army was able to overcome Jabin's capital, Hazor, and defeat the occupying Canaanites.

GIDEON AND THE SWORD OF THE LORD

Free of the Canaanite gods, the Israelites now seemed to search for other idols to worship. Baal, of the Midianites, became very popular in the Promised Land and altars were built all over the country. The town of Ophrah, about thirty miles north of Jerusalem, where a young man called Gideon resided, was the site of such an altar.

The Midianites hailed from the Arabian desert, and they came in vast hordes with their camels and tents, invading Israel with 135,000 armed men (Judg. 8:10). They were like grasshoppers, stripping the planted fields as soon as there was a crop. Northern Israel was close to famine. Finally, the people prayed to the Lord —not to Baal—for a deliverer. In answer, God sent forth the cautious Gideon.

Gideon was secretly threshing wheat in a field (lest the Midianites catch him) when an angel appeared to him and commissioned him to save Israel from the occupiers (Judg. 6:11). Gideon, not one to become overly excited just because he sees an angel, complains that he is just a poor country boy, and might he have a sign from Heaven? He prepares a meal for the angel, who then touches the food with his staff and burns it up in flames like an offering. Impressed, Gideon now builds an altar for the Lord at that spot, calling it Jehovah-Shalom.

That night, under God's direction, Gideon knocked down his father Joash's altar to Baal and chopped up the wooden idols that were with it. He then made a sacrifice to the Lord on the wreckage. When the men awoke, they were ready to kill Gideon, but Joash protected him, and said, "Let Baal defend himself—it was his altar" (Judg. 6:32).

Gideon then sent for certain of the tribes to gather for fighting —Manasseh, Asher, Zebulun, and Naphtali. He did not extend the invitation to Ephraim, which they later resented (Judg. 8:1). Gideon now requested a further sign from the Lord, and "put out the fleece" (Judg. 6:37-40).

Thus fortified with his latest sign, Gideon confronted his thirty-two thousand troops. The tribes had responded well with soldiers, but the Lord was of the opinion that Gideon had too many. They would boast that it was their own victory if they came in such strength, the Lord felt (Judg. 7:2). In point of fact, they were outnumbered four to one, as things stood, but Gideon felt obliged to reduce the army. Rather like today's U. S. Marines, he began looking for "a few good men."

First, Gideon asked all of those who were scared to leave. Twenty-two thousand soldiers obliged him immediately! He put the remaining ten thousand to a test of alertness at a river. Those who put their faces in the water to drink were eliminated; those who lifted the water to their mouths, never looking down, were enlisted. The latter were considered much more skillful soldiers.

But Gideon found himself with a mere three hundred men.

Now God provided Gideon a further reassuring sign. The Lord told him to sneak into the Midianite encampment in the Valley of Jezreel in order to estimate the morale of the enemy. Gideon overheard two Midianite soldiers discussing the coming battle. One said he had a dream in which a loaf of barley bread rolled into the army of Midian and knocked a tent flat. The other said that meant Gideon would defeat the Midianites. Naturally, Gideon was thrilled to hear this. The vast army of the Midianites was mentally prepared for defeat.

Gideon had finally seen enough signs and now prepared to attack. He ingeniously placed three companies of a hundred men on the surrounding hillsides about the massive Midian camp. At a given signal in the middle of the night, each man broke a clay jar, exposing an oil lamp within, and blew a trumpet shouting, "The sword of the Lord, and of Gideon!" (Judg. 7:20).

The confused Midianites must have thought there were hundreds of thousands of troops all over the hills, and they began running about in the dark, killing each other. Gideon was able to cut through them over and over again, and slew 120,000 men that night. He later pursued the rest across the Jordan, where he and his enlarged army killed them to the last man (Judg. 8:28).

(This particular battle has been compared to the 1967 war, almost in the same sector, when the Israelis dropped barrels of heating oil, set afire, from airplanes, confusing the defenders of the Golan Heights and routing the Syrians.)

Israel gained peace for another forty years.

SUPERMAN

Near the end of the theocracy of Judges, there appears a re-markable man who is one of the best known of the Bible—Samson. His name ranks with Hercules, Atlas, and the modern-day Superman in the literature of the whole world. In modern Israel, the best-advertised tires are called "*Shimshon*", or "Samson" tires.

The enemy this time were the tenacious Philistines, a sea-faring people with the technological advantage of sources of iron and the ability to make it into weapons. In a bronze age, iron is king, and the Philistines, skillful with their forges, led the arms race of their day. They were extremely idolatrous people, worshipping the fish god, Dagon, and were very licentious in their worship, employing temple prostitutes. They gave their pervasive name "Palestine" to the Promised Land.

They liked to live along the coastland of Israel, and they made steady war with the Hebrews from this point on, until they were finally eliminated by the invincible David.

Samson's birth was somewhat like Isaac's, in that he came as his mother's first child, late in the lives of his parents, according to the promise of an angel. The boy was to take a Nazarite vow, meaning that he was not to drink alcoholic beverages and he was never to shave his head or facial hair (Num. 6:5; Judg. 13:5). During the prenatal period, his mother was not to drink wine, either. The angel announced the heartening news that this child would deliver Israel from the Philistines.

When he was of age, Samson spied an unnamed but beautiful Philistine girl at Timnah, and it was love at first sight. He told his father he wished to marry her, and got the angry retort, "What a start for someone who is going to deliver Israel from the Philistines!" We can hear that plaintive cry, "Can't you find a Hebrew girl?"

On a trip to Timnah to see his fiancee, Samson was attacked by a lion, but the incredibly strong young man killed the beast with his bare hands. On a later trip, he saw the lion's skeleton with honey in it, produced by bees who had built a hive. He had some of the honey as refreshment and thought about the irony of a lion producing honey.

Samson's parents were obliged to arrange a wedding feast for him and his bride, and the Timnites invited thirty Philistine men to the celebration.

Teetotaler that he was, Samson had a bit of a gambler's streak and made a wager with the wedding guests. If they could figure out a riddle he would pose in seven days, he would give them thirty suits of clothes (Judg. 14:14). If they couldn't, they would present him the same—a very nice wardrobe for a bridegroom. The Philistines agreed, and Samson proposed the following riddle: "Out of the eater comes food, out of the strong comes sweetness."

The foreigners were stymied for an answer, but they got Samson's bride to one side and badgered her to question him about it privately. Finally, the answer came out of him (Samson's legendary weakness was pretty Philistine girls). The solution, of course, was Samson's peculiar encounter with the lion—the eater which gave forth food, and the strong out of which came sweetness.

After the bride told the thirty wedding guests, Samson coined the quaint phrase, "If you had not plowed with my heifer, you had not found out my riddle" (Judg. 14:18).

Obliged to pay off his debt, Samson made a side trip to the Philistine city of Ashkelon, killed thirty men in hand-to-hand combat, and brought their suits back to his creditors.

But, in the meanwhile, the bride's father took the opportunity to give the girl to one of the wedding guests. Infuriated, Samson tied torches on the tails of three hundred foxes and sent them through the wheat fields, vineyards, and olive groves of the Philistines, burning them up. The affected farmers retaliated by killing the bride and father. Then, in counter revenge, Samson killed all of them. Samson was becoming quite a nuisance around the Philistine territories.

Now the Philistines organized a thousand-man regiment, and asked the people of Judah to extradite Samson, since he was now residing in Judah. The Judahites fearfully approached the mighty one, but he said it would be perfectly all right for them to bind him and hand him over to the enemy. As he was handed over, however, the power of God came upon Samson, who burst his ropes and grabbed the nearest weapon—a donkey's jawbone—and faced the thousand-man regiment bearing the dreaded iron weapons. No Philistine survived.

Seemingly invincible, Samson now met his match—the Philistine beauty of Sorek—Delilah. There are very few girls named Delilah or Jezebel these days, for good reason. The Philistine leaders, realizing Samson's soft spot, offered Delilah eleven hundred silver pieces to ascertain the secret of the great strength of this ancient-day, six-million-dollar man. The secret was his long hair, of course.

Samson couldn't seem to stand a woman's constant questions. He didn't really want to tell her, but finally he did. At first, he said that green vines would bind him. While he slept, Delilah tied him with green vines, but he snapped them upon awakening—to the chagrin of the waiting Philistine soldiers. Next, they tried the same thing with new ropes, and then, getting warmer, tied his hair in a web. Finally, the truth came out and Samson's Nazarite vow was violated when Delilah arranged to have his hair cut. The Philistines attacked the shorn Samson, found him helpless, bound him, blinded him, and put him to work in a prison grinding grain with a millstone. In time, Samson repented and gradually his hair grew back.

In one of the scenes that make Bible movies what they are, the Philistines decided to have a mammoth victory celebration over the downfall of that dreaded Judge of Israel. The massive Dagon Temple was the site of this landmark occasion, and three thousand men and women came out to humiliate Samson. He was paraded before them as a blind, stumbling fool.

Samson asked a boy to position him by the main structural pillars of the temple, and, while everyone was deep in revelry, he uttered a fervent prayer for one last gift of strength from the Lord. And then, with one mighty push on the pillars, Samson threw down the enormous temple, killing all three thousand Philistines and himself as well (Judg. 16:30).

In his volatile career, he had judged Israel twenty years, and he was taken back by the Hebrews and buried in his father's graveyard. The point was not missed, undoubtedly, by the Hebrews or the Philistines, that Samson's wondrous strength lay not particularly in his hair, or even in his body, but in his faith in the God of Israel. He died a righteous man, showing in his last earthly act the full power of Jehovah against the idolaters.

THE CONVERT

The little Book of Ruth presents a story of Gentile conversion to the Jewish faith. Ruth was a Moabitess who married an Israelite named Elimelech. She became a widow at a young age, however, and accompanied her mother-in-law, Naomi, to Israel, settling in Elimelech's former home, Bethlehem (Ruth 1:16).

Ruth and Naomi were very poor, and were obliged to eat what they could glean from the corners of the local barley fields. According to the law given on Sinai, farmers were to leave the corners of their fields for the poor (Lev. 23:22). Gleaning in the field of Boaz one day, Ruth meets the unmarried wealthy owner. Boaz, a cousin of Elimelech, is rather taken with the poverty stricken young beauty. He tells his men to make sure she is treated well throughout the harvest. When Naomi hears the good news, she is ecstatic and begins to plot toward a match.

Naomi taught the unlearned Ruth the Jewish law, particularly emphasizing that a kinsman of a deceased Hebrew must marry his childless widow in order to raise up descendants for him (Deut. 25:5–10). The woman did the courting in this situation; Ruth was to sleep at Boaz's feet—a tacit formal request for marriage and fulfillment of the law. Ruth went out looking for Boaz, found him threshing barley by himself, and kept an eye on him. When he tired and lay down to sleep, she carried out her part of the law. When Boaz woke up at midnight, he was pleasantly surprised by the pretty girl at his feet—and especially that she had chosen him, instead of one of the younger men. He told her that he would be happy to marry her, even though he was not the nearest relative. He indicated that that situation could be handled.

The next day, the influential Boaz went to court, summoning the nearest relative and ten witnesses. Boaz challenged the relative —Elimelech had left a debt; there was a vacant lot to be re-

deemed. The relative said he would purchase it. Then Boaz said
the man would have to take Elimelech's widow, as well, and raise
up descendants for him. Outbidded, the relative declined, took off
a shoe and gave it to Boaz (according to Mosaic law). Boaz asked
the ten men to witness the action and announced that he himself
would take Ruth to wife and buy the land. His adversary, glad to
get out of the proceedings at the cost of one shoe, hobbled home
gratefully.

Boaz and Ruth made a happy couple, and quite a significant
one. They became the grandparents of one of Israel's superlative
men, King David.

6

God Saved the King:
David Reigns in Israel

Here is flesh and blood! Here is passion, talent, accomplishment, faith! Here is David—musician, poet, warrior, adulterer—King of the Jews for forty prosperous years.

Here is a real-life character before whom the heroes of the pagan legends fade into inconsequential myth.

Weep with this mighty sovereign as his sons die, at birth, and in open rebellion against the throne. Confess with him his heinous sins. Walk with him humbly, as he did before the prophet Samuel. Praise God with him in his deathless Psalms.

Honored by God in the opening breath of the New Testament ("The book of the generation of Jesus Christ, the son of David . . ."), this King stands dominant in the center of the Old Testament. Were it not for his equally illustrious son Solomon, David would unquestionably represent the very definition of what was the King of the Jews until the coming of the Messiah Himself.

He lies enshrined to this day on Mount Zion in Jerusalem, the capital he established for God. Citizens of all nations stand in awe at the tomb of the splendid David, dead three thousand years but still the inspiration of Bible students the world over, Jew and Gentile together.

The majesty of his writings, the fearsomeness of his armies, the skill of his administration of Israel changed the history of the world and advanced the plan of God for men. He came to power in a warring, quarrelsome time for his nation, succeeding a weak and even maddened King Saul, but he left Israel at the pinnacle of its nationhood.

It is fair to say that Israel has never again achieved the might, the power, the reverence, and the sovereignty among nations that was enjoyed under King David.

And yet his story opens on a quiet pasture near the little hamlet of Bethlehem, where the boy David tended his father's sheep.

David did well to survive until he was called to be King, considering the despotic jealousy of the deteriorating Saul. Saul had been anointed before the birth of David and had ruled troubled Israel competently, distinguishing himself on the omnipresent battlefields of the Holy Land. But by the time David had reached adolescence it became clear that something was very much the matter with the King.

Saul began to disobey the instructions of God, given plainly through the prophet Samuel. He grew indolent in his power, unmindful of his solemn spiritual responsibilities and terribly jealous of the young David. He ended his days in a relentless, paranoid passion to destroy David, whose imminent ascension to the throne of Israel grew ever more apparent.

Seven centuries before David's time, Jacob had prophesied that Judah would be the royal tribe, but during that period no one from Judah ruled over Israel. Moses was of the Tribe of Levi, Joshua was of Ephraim, and the Judges were from various tribes, but not Judah. When the people yearned for their first King, God selected Saul from the Tribe of Benjamin.

Why was the royal tribe excluded from leadership all this time?

Some suggest it had to do with a prohibition the Lord gave in the Law of Moses: "A bastard shall not enter the congregation of the Lord; even to his tenth generation shall he not enter into the congregation of the Lord" (Deut. 23:2). In the remarkable chapter, Genesis 38, the story is told of how Judah had twin sons by his widowed daughter-in-law, Tamar, who posed as a prostitute to entrap the indiscreet Judah. Thus, ten full generations would have to pass before a descendant of Judah could be a leader in Israel, by the letter of the Law. In the Book of Ruth, we read that there were exactly ten generations from Judah's son Perez to David (Ruth 4:18–22). Could it be that the Lord was waiting until David's generation to anoint a leader for Israel out of the royal Tribe of Judah?

DAVID THE SHEPHERD

It would certainly have been hard to picture the teenage shepherd boy David—a poet, a dreamer, a composer of sweet songs to God—as the mighty sovereign of the chosen people that he was to become according to the Will of God. The promises had been made earlier, as we have seen, as to the particular line out of which God would select the coming King, but David wouldn't have seemed a likely prospect.

As he strummed away the pastoral days on his little harp and tended his father's flocks, David gathered little in the way of combat experience. He protected his sheep against the predatory animals of the Judean Hills, but this hardly qualified him to one day face the invincible Goliath.

Still, God had marked him out. Samuel arrived one day at the simple home of Jesse with instructions from God to anoint the next King of all Israel.

Jesse the sheep farmer must have been overwhelmed. It is not clear whether he understood the ancient prophecy singling out his tribe as the royal line, but he certainly cooperated with the prophet. Having eight sons he had many suggestions as to a likely King.

Jesse's recommendations included his seven older boys but David was not mentioned. Probably it was not just his youth but also his simple ways that disqualified David in his father's mind. People accustomed to seeing the warrior Saul at the head of Israel's deadly armies just didn't think in terms of daydreaming shepherds for the job. The youngest boy was left to his music and his flocks by his father.

But the word of the Lord was most explicit. Samuel called for David. Before his astonished family, David was anointed by the respected prophet. The shepherd boy was to be King.

DAVID THE SOLDIER

It must not have been very clear as to just how this simple country lad was to ascend to the throne, but the Lord arranged a way for David to come to the attention of all Israel.

The story of David and Goliath bears repeating even after some three thousand years of beloved familiarity and endless quotation in favor of almost any underdog. Israel was at war as usual, with the determined Saul at his customary post at the front, when a stalemate occurred. The Israelites and the Philistines had fought to a standstill. And the mighty Goliath came forward with a proposition.

Goliath the giant, fully nine feet tall, offered himself as the champion of the Philistines; he would fight any champion of the Israelites personally. The war would be decided on this one-against-one basis.

We must appreciate the position of Saul on this unique matter. He simply could not reject the challenge; that would seem cowardly. On the other hand, where would he find a match for Goliath? We can safely assume that volunteers were lacking. But the loss of this war would mean the ruination of Saul's kingdom.

At length Saul opted to accept the challenge. And as the fate of all Israel hung in the balance he searched through his army for an undiscovered Samson. The weeks passed, we should appreciate, as the mightiest warriors of Israel kept clear of the glance of the King.

Goliath enjoyed himself. He took considerable delight in the situation, chiding the Israelites daily, ho-humming about the field. His confidence was overwhelming, his derision utterly galling.

It's interesting to note that the tall, strong Saul never considered taking on Goliath himself. Neither did he consult the Lord about the problem, according to the record. Samuel was on the scene and available to Saul also, but the King fretted about, solitary in his decision.

And finally David arrived. We can imagine the incredulous reaction of the King and the assembled might of Israel as the youngster stepped forward with his two weapons—a sling shot and perfect faith in the God of Israel.

It is distinctly clear in the text that David relied on the Lord. He was perfectly confident of victory because he considered Jehovah more powerful than the gods of the Philistines. He was completely convinced that this particular bout would be decided not on the human level, where the result seemed abundantly predictable, but on the supernatural level. The fight would be about who was God and who was not God, David felt.

He felled Goliath with one stone and decapitated the mammoth with his own sword. The appalled Philistines withdrew and David of Bethlehem was a national hero.

King Saul was impressed, and very grateful, to say the least. David was honored with a commission and eventually rose to the rank of captain in Israel's armed forces. The shepherd-poet proved to be an excellent soldier and gathered many successes in the field.

From Saul's point of view David became *too* good a soldier. It was being whispered about the land, "Saul has killed thousands, but David has killed ten thousand!" Saul failed to value this distinction and the aging warrior slowly began a vendetta against his former champion. The seeds of jealousy grew until Saul, in his fury, sought to kill the champion who had saved Israel.

DAVID THE OUTLAW

Saul declared David an outlaw. He was to be hunted down and destroyed!

The young future King was obliged to go into hiding in the land he helped to preserve. Ironically, he was forewarned of Saul's plan by Saul's own son, the natural successor to the throne, Jonathan. Contemporaries, David and Jonathan were close friends, and the "crown prince" could not abide his father's murderous ways.

At Jonathan's warning David took to the hills around the Dead Sea, very near Masada, where the last of the Israelites vanquished by the Romans in the first century A.D. sought refuge. It's hard, unforgiving country, arid and wild. David was able to elude Saul's police.

For years the hunt went on, as the anointed of God evaded certain death at the hands of his own government. David was able to assemble around him a following of sundry men who opposed Saul's policies as he went, and eventually he formed a small but effective army of his own. David's vigilantes faithfully fought the enemies of Israel on the borders as an unauthorized militia of fugitives, in what must be a most remarkable example of patriotism in action.

The regular Israeli forces fought a tragic battle in the northern area, meanwhile, and both Saul and Jonathan were killed in action. The nation was without a monarch or a successor.

Shortly God's plan for David was fully realized. He was the logical contender for the throne by this time and he soon became the undisputed King of all Israel.

ON TO JERUSALEM

David ruled at first from Hebron, in the southern part of Judah, but the strategically placed Jerusalem appealed to him as a better capital. More central, and situated on unusually high ground, the ancient city held many advantages. David was ultimately able to capture Jerusalem from the Jebusites, who controlled it at the time, and he moved the seat of Israeli government to where it now stands today.

To assess the rule of David in a few words is wholly unfair and not really possible, but suffice it to say that he utterly reorganized his nation and brought it to its all-time greatest fruition. He united the twelve tribes into one strong entity, he subdued or pacified all of the Canaanite enemies of Israel throughout the land, he established advantageous and mutually profitable relations with the surrounding nations, and he brought the worship of God to a hearty, flourishing level.

The people of Israel became inspired. Their leader was clearly, as the Scriptures attest, "A man after God's own heart." The King loved God, he constantly sought after God, and he was always

motivated by and deeply concerned about the heartfelt, sponta-
neous worship of the Lord God of Israel.

His skill as a musician had only grown greater as he matured,
and the former composer of the Judean fields went on to create a
massive musical literature of praise to God, unequaled in all the
holy books of the world. His songs of worship and spiritual reali-
zation were carefully codified in the Book of Psalms. They were
sung by the magnificent male choir of the Tabernacle at Shiloh,
and later at the Temple of God in Jerusalem. It is probable that a
majority of the 150 timeless Psalms of the Bible, which bring inspiration of a kind unique even to Scripture, were written and
composed by King David.

They are perhaps his most pristine legacy. They are the mightiest of all of his mighty works.

ADULTERER AND MURDERER

With all of his allegiance to God and with his lifetime's experience in seeing the reality of God's power, David was still a common sinner like any one of us. In fact, it can be fairly said that
David was an *un*common sinner; few of us would combine
murder with adultery, as he did, to satisfy a passing lust.

His reign and his personality were greatly marred by this excess.
It seems that David spied the beautiful Bathsheba from his palace
roof garden; she was bathing, and the King was overcome with
desire for her.

Bathsheba was the Hebrew wife of a trusted Hittite, Uriah,
whom David had elevated to the rank of captain in his army.
Uriah was away at war, defending Israel, and the King stooped to
adultery with his wife. Bathsheba became pregnant and the two
conspired to have it appear that the child in her womb was
Uriah's, but this failed. Ultimately David "put out a contract" on
poor Uriah, causing him to be isolated at the front and killed in
action.

Naturally the plotting attracted some attention; some of David's troops had to be let in on the King's solution to his dilemma.
Within a few months the reputation of the former savior of Israel

was deeply tainted and King David was confronted by a prophet of God. Utterly compromised, the crestfallen sovereign confessed his gross sin to the Lord, and God graciously forgave the error.

But David's crime would follow him to the grave nevertheless. His child with Bathsheba died at birth, and the pages of the Old Testament are nowhere more pitiful than in the recorded prayers and fastings of the King in hopeless petition for the life of this child. David did take Bathsheba then as his rightful wife and Queen, and their later son, Solomon, became heir to the throne.

But another son, Absalom, revolted against his father, leading an armed rebellion against the throne and causing Israel terrible civil strife and grief. David's armies met Absalom's renegades successfully and the rebel prince was killed in battle.

David was inconsolable. "Would God I had died for thee," he wept over Absalom. David's tragedy is complete with this latter loss of a son and the reader's heart is torn by the pathos in the record.

Neither David nor his kingdom ever overcame the sad results of his lapse into degradation.

THE TEMPLE OF GOD

But great joys and expectations also accompanied the long career of King David. The best of these was the anticipation of David's building a true Temple of God in Jerusalem.

The Almighty had dwelt among His people in the Tabernacle while they wandered in the wilderness. And for the four hundred years since the time of Moses the Tabernacle was still Israel's holy place, being established at Shiloh, fifteen miles north of the capital. But now Jerusalem was secure and the splendid Mount Moriah was available to the Jews. This singular site was the very mountain where Abraham had willingly come forth to sacrifice Isaac almost a thousand years before. How appropriate a place for Israel to continue her obedience toward God in sacrificial worship.

David, who had achieved peace with Israel's enemies, built the national treasury and constructed a mighty palace for himself, now regretted that the House of God was "within curtains" while he himself "dwelt in a house of cedar." Surely a more fitting place could now be established for God. The time was right and the place was right.

But the King wasn't "right." The prophet Nathan came forth with the disheartening news that, while God approved of the idea of building the Temple, David wasn't the one to do it. There was blood on David's hands, Nathan pointed out. He had slain many men. It would be more fitting that the House of God be built by a man of peace. And so David's son, Solomon, whose name derives from the Hebrew word *shalom*, meaning "peace," would be appointed to the sacred task.

David had a good attitude toward this disappointment and busied himself gathering the prodigious materials for the massive construction job and instructing his son in the holiness of the undertaking. It should be appreciated that King David spent many happy years just organizing this gigantic project.

THE ETERNAL DYNASTY

David's last days were greatly gladdened by a stunning promise of God about his dynasty. What father does not have concern about the welfare of his children, grandchildren, and ongoing posterity—particularly when that father is King?

History had already taught that royal families die off or are removed by force from their rule. David had witnessed the early death of his dear friend Jonathan, the heir to Saul's throne. How would his own son Solomon fare, and what about Solomon's sons?

Well, God's promise really underwrote the royal dynasty of Israel. God promised to David a covenant that had never been made, and has never since been made, with any King of any nation. The implications are astounding:

And thine house and thy kingdom shall be established for ever before thee: thy throne shall be established for ever. (II Sam. 7:16)

David's royal line would last *forever*, God said!
Now there's a covenant to perk up the spirits of any King!

There's a promise you can live with! David would never lack an heir to sit on his throne and there would *always* be a descendant of David qualified to rule from Jerusalem!

Of course the covenant referred to the Messianic promise that had descended already from the patriarchs and Judah. We will explain the progression more fully in Part Two of this book. The Messiah, of the Tribe of Judah and the royal line of King David, shall rule in Jerusalem forever. "The sceptre shall not depart from Judah," God had promised solemnly.

David went to his grave with that one-of-a-kind covenant ringing in his ears, and with the sure knowledge that what he had started out to accomplish—the true sanctification of Israel (and even the whole world)—would continue on after him through his heirs.

There were few personalities like David in history. His example of utter faith in God, and stumbling as well, serves as a true-to-life lesson in the human condition still today.

The world has not yet seen Israel rise again to the heights achieved by this remarkable shepherd-King, but according to God's promise, it will.

7

Solomon in All His Glory:
The Temple of God

He was one of the most gifted and accomplished men ever to grace a throne. His keen perceptions and marvelous insights come down to us in some of the most majestic writing of the Old Testament.

He was a man of great passion; he composed the Song of Solomon. He was a man of subtle wisdom; he authored the Book of Proverbs. He was a man of unfathomable depth; he wrote the profound Book of Ecclesiastes.

An administrator of consummate skill, he kept the peace, multiplied the wealth of Israel, and adorned Jerusalem with the Temple of God. His intellect, his wealth, and his utter debauchery, are all overwhelming. It is fair to say that, in so many ways, the world has never seen another Solomon.

THE PRICE OF MONARCHY

Along with Kings come battles for the throne. Solomon's ascension was as hazardous as his father's before him.

It was around 960 B.C., and David had succeeded in uniting the twelve tribes of Israel firmly under his own rule. He had defeated or neutralized all of the primary enemies of the Hebrew nation, and, in his old age, designated his son, Solomon, by Bathsheba, to be his heir to the throne. But Solomon's brother, Adonijah, seeing his opportunity, attempted to seize the crown by a coup. King David was practically on his deathbed, "old and stricken in years;

and they covered him with clothes, but he gat no heat" (I Kings 1:1). On that occasion, the servants of the King sought to warm the ailing monarch by means of a beautiful young virgin, "And the damsel was very fair, and cherished the king, and ministered to him: but the king knew her not" (I Kings 1:4).

Not really very moved by the grave condition of the King, Adonijah invited the political and military leaders of Israel to a great banquet, while David lay suffering and impotent. But the loyal prophet Nathan, along with Bathsheba, revealed the intrigue to the King, and David ordered the immediate public anointing of Solomon at the Gihon Spring by Jerusalem. The priesthood and the people at large rallied behind Solomon, and Adonijah fled to the Tabernacle altar for sanctuary.

The banquet was certainly ruined:

And all the guests that were with Adonijah were afraid, and rose up, and went every man his way.

And Adonijah feared because of Solomon, and arose, and went, and caught hold on the horns of the altar.

And it was told Solomon, saying, Behold, Adonijah fearest king Solomon: for, lo, he hath caught hold on the horns of the altar, saying, Let king Solomon swear unto me to day that he will not slay his servant with the sword. (I Kings 1:49–51)

Solomon reacted commendably in his first kingly deed:

And Solomon said, If he will shew himself a worthy man, there shall not an hair of him fall to the earth: but if wickedness shall be found in him, he shall die. (I Kings 1:52)

Soon after, Solomon attended his father's deathbed and heard the final words of David to his favored son. David admonished the new young King to be steadfast in the ways of the Lord, and also to take courage in the marvelous commission of building the Temple of God.

And thou, Solomon my son, know thou the God of thy father, and serve him with a perfect heart and with a willing mind: for the Lord searcheth all hearts, and understandeth all the imaginations of the thoughts: if thou seek him, he will be found of thee; but if thou forsake him, he will cast thee off for ever.

Take heed now; for the Lord hath chosen thee to build an house for the sanctuary: be strong, and do it. (I Chron. 28:9–10)

But Solomon found it necessary to spend his first few years strengthening his control over the throne by purging the land of many of his own and his father's antagonists. Adonijah had not quite given up his aspirations and hatched a subtle plot, asking for the hand of the very damsel that had been brought to cheer the ailing David. Solomon was as good as his earlier promise, and executed Adonijah, along with the military leader Joab, who had taken part in the plot.

A PRAYER FOR WISDOM

King Solomon already had enough wisdom to ask the Lord for more. His throne was now secure, but he realized that guiding the Chosen People would call for great understanding. Solomon prayed with humility:

And now, O Lord my God, thou hast made thy servant king instead of David my father: and I am but a little child: I know not how to go out or come in.

And thy servant is in the midst of thy people which thou hast chosen, a great people, that cannot be numbered nor counted for multitude.

Give therefore thy servant an understanding heart to judge thy people, that I may discern between good and bad: for who is able to judge this thy so great a people? (I Kings 3:7–9)

God's reaction must have overwhelmed the humble one:

And the speech pleased the Lord, that Solomon had asked this thing.

And God said unto him, Because thou hast asked this thing, and hast not asked for thyself long life; neither hast asked riches for thyself, nor hast asked the life of thine enemies; but hast asked for thyself understanding to discern judgment;

Behold, I have done according to thy words: lo, I have given thee a wise and an understanding heart; so that there was none like thee before thee, neither after thee shall any arise like unto thee. (I Kings 3:10–12)

Furthermore, God went on to grant riches, "so that there shall not be any among the kings like unto thee all thy days"; and, also, longevity ("I will lengthen thy days"). Thus, God granted Solomon's original entreaty and more besides.

Solomon went on to prove out his answered prayer. The story of the two harlot mothers, both claiming a single baby, is very well known. The King advised that the baby be cut in half, and each woman take her share. One mother agreed; the other tearfully said it would be better to give the child to her adversary. The King thus discerned that the child belonged to the latter.

His administrative wisdom was the equal of his father's, with perhaps a greater measure of fiscal skill. Solomon divided his kingdom into twelve districts, roughly along the tribal lines, and appointed governors, who oversaw the contributions of produce for the royal court. Military garrisons were established liberally throughout the land and on the frontiers—always a good idea in Israel. Forty-thousand horse stalls and twelve thousand horsemen provided a standing militia.

Solomon valued education and was, himself, something of a genius (I Kings 4:29–34). The King's creative works were prolific. He produced three thousand proverbs, many being inspired of God and incorporated into the Book of Proverbs; he composed one thousand and five songs; he was an expert in botany and zoology. The King of Israel enjoyed a just reputation for high culture, from Egypt to Babylonia. The ancient Greeks had not, as yet, risen on the world scene when Solomon began conducting his scientific experiments and composing his brilliant poetry and music.

THE TEMPLE

But his masterpiece was the House of God.

It had been in the mind of his father to build a permanent structure of fitting grandeur, wherein the precious artifacts of the portable Tabernacle could be kept forever, but God had ruled that there was too much blood on David's hands. The Temple would, instead, be built by this man of peace, Solomon. And so now Solomon set about one of the most prodigious building projects of his time.

The Holy Temple of Jerusalem, a major theme of the entire Bible (and the future, as well, according to prophecy), is synonymous with the name of Solomon. When the crusaders were to arrive in Israel some two thousand years later and discover the magnificent Moslem Dome of the Rock, they mistakenly assumed that it was Solomon's Temple and dubbed it "Templum Domini" —the Temple of the Lord. Its splendor seemed representative to them of the mighty Solomon.

The first problem was timber—never very abundant in the Holy Land. Solomon already had much of the gold and silver that his father had gathered for this project, but massive amounts of lumber were needed.

Solomon negotiated a complex agreement with his friend, King Hiram of Tyre, to provide the fabled cedars of Lebanon. Solomon would provide Hebrew laborers and would pay the local overseers and skilled workmen. Hiram would transport the gigantic trees down from Mount Lebanon to Tyre, and place them on ships bound for an Israeli port. Solomon would pay Hiram about a thousand pounds of wheat and fifty gallons of pure olive oil every year for the rest of Hiram's life.

The massive stones for the Temple, some of which still stand in the Western Wall in Jerusalem, were cut out of a nearby Jerusalem quarry. Israel does have plenty of stone, and there was no need to import it. But there was one difficult requirement; all stone-fitting had to be done at the quarry. God would brook no hammering and chiseling at His holy site (I Kings 6:7).

It took seven years to build the great Temple (I Kings 6:38), but when it was finally finished, it was a wonder of the ancient world. The splendor of the finest stone, cedar, gold and silver, lavishly spread over fully thirty-four acres, overwhelmed all who toured Jerusalem.

Solomon's magnificent sermon and prayer of dedication, covering a full Biblical chapter (II Chron. 6), represents a landmark in Old Testament entreaty to God. Solomon had brought 142,000 animals to sacrifice (II Chron. 7:5), and dedicated the House of God in matchless words of oblation.

The Lord was very pleased with the Temple and the dedication prayer, and filled the building with the Shekinah Glory Cloud, which had also attended the Tabernacle in the wilderness. The priests were unable to stay in the building in the presence of the Cloud:

> And it came to pass, when the priests were come out of the holy *place*, that the cloud filled the house of the Lord,
>
> So that the priests could not stand to minister because of the cloud: for the glory of the Lord had filled the house of the Lord. (I Kings 8:10–11)

THE QUEEN OF SHEBA

The Queen of Sheba has enjoyed an undeserved three-thousand-year reputation as the wife or lover of King Solomon. Actually, Solomon, definitely the marrying kind, had seven hundred wives (plus three hundred concubines), but the Queen of Sheba was not one of them.

She had merely decided to come to Israel to see for herself the remarkable Solomon, whose wondrous Temple and magnificent court was now spoken of in awe throughout the known world. As one successful monarch to another, the Queen of Sheba had come to pay her respects and perhaps gain a word from the wise.

Sheba was an east African or, perhaps, an Arabian country some eight hundred miles from Israel. The Queen gladly undertook this arduous journey, and was certainly not disappointed by Israel, the showplace of the Middle East.

What seemed to impress her the most was the stunning pageantry and golden resplendence of Solomon's palace, and the marvelous beauty of worship in the Temple, complete with the all-male Levitical choir performing the Psalms of King David (I Kings 10:4–9; II Chron. 9:1–8).

Apparently, the Queen had an amicable visit with Solomon, but there is no mention of a romantic liaison in the Scriptural record. The legendary love affair was supposed to have produced the royal line of Ethiopia, so that Haile Selassie claimed the remarkable title, "Lion of the Tribe of Judah."

It is certainly a tribute to Solomon that the Queen of Sheba would come such a distance to attend, as it were, a workshop on how to manage a kingdom.

IDOLATRY IN THE ROYAL PALACE

Somewhere during Solomon's long reign of forty years, he began to lose his grip. From the pinnacle of spiritual, intellectual, and administrative glory he had achieved, he somehow began to descend.

Dallying endlessly with his prodigious collection of wives and mistresses, the once greatly admired monarch of the Holy Land began to draw glances across every border. While his kingdom did not weaken, he began to accumulate a number of powerful enemies. Edom, on the east, and Syria, on the northern border, were particularly strong in those times.

The cause of it all was Solomon's departure from the Lord, according to the Scriptures. When he began to marry non-Israelite women, ostensibly at first for diplomatic reasons, his faith went to pieces. He married princesses of Egypt, Moab, Ammon, Edom, Sidon, and so forth, to cultivate valuable alliances, but, eventually, this diplomatic technique got completely out of hand. Solomon's enormous harem finally turned him away from spiritual pursuits, as we may well imagine, and it all ended with the disgusting spectacle of the Godly King who had built the Jerusalem Temple actually constructing centers of worship for pagan deities (I Kings 11:3–8).

The idolatry of the King inevitably spread through the land, weakening the spiritual base of Israel and greatly angering the Lord. The King found himself ensnared in a pantheon of false gods as the united Kingdom of Israel deteriorated.

Solomon died in dishonor, deeply disappointing his millions of subjects and the long-suffering God of Israel.

8

The Captains and the Kings:
A Nation Divided

Solomon bequeathed to his nation his two most outstanding characteristics: the righteousness that had made Israel mighty and the miserable paganism that brought her low.

Somehow these two opposing traits were replete in the same personality, and the chosen people now became a nation of Solomons. Vigorous faith in God went on in great measure, while the cancer of idolatry spread ominously throughout the land.

THE SCORPION KING

Now Israel was coming apart. In the times of the Judges, the nation was a shaky alliance of twelve loosely knit tribes. During the 120 years or so under Saul, David, and Solomon, it had become a united kingdom of great strength. But now there was talk of secession of the northern ten tribes, and eventually the country became divided and fatally weakened.

The southern two tribes adhered to Jerusalem, and the northern ten tribes created Shechem and, later, Samaria as their capital. For the next three centuries, under a succession of Kings of varying competence and spiritual persuasions, Israel deteriorated.

In the very last days of Solomon, when the nearly demented King seemed to live out frantically his timeless philosophy, "Vanity of vanities, all is vanity," a pretender to the throne arose. Jeroboam, who was one of Solomon's governors, received the inspiration to organize the ten northern tribes into a separate kingdom. The prophet Ahijah of Shiloh had given Jeroboam a fateful message. Ahijah met the governor on the highway coming out of Jerusalem, and dramatically rent his garment, tearing it into twelve pieces. He indicated that Jeroboam should take ten of the pieces, signifying that the governor would become King over ten of the tribes. The two pieces left would represent Judah and one other tribe, which would remain faithful to the Davidic dynasty for King David's sake. The prophet promised that if Jeroboam would be faithful to the Lord, his dynasty would be like David's—that is, perpetual. God was doing this because of Solomon's apostasy, the prophet advised.

Jeroboam was certainly impressed, but the news of this disconcerting prophecy got back to King Solomon, who immediately published a death warrant against Jeroboam. The governor was forced to flee to Egypt for sanctuary.

After Solomon's death, his son Rehoboam ascended to the throne. His mother was an Ammonitess, one of Solomon's preferred foreign wives.

The new King had inherited everything of his father's but his wisdom. He liked his father's policies of heavy labor on the part of the common folk for the profit of the palace, and he proceeded impatiently to have himself inaugurated in grand style. He traveled to Shechem, in central Israel, and arranged for all twelve tribes to swear allegiance to him there.

A bit circumspect, the tribes recalled Jeroboam from Egypt and he became their spokesman. The respected former governor stood on a platform of reduction in taxes, and especially in the forced labor. Solomon had accomplished his magnificent building programs and vast wealth mainly on the mandatory service of the crown on the part of the entire populace. The populist Jeroboam took a stand that guaranteed him the favor of the common people at large.

Rehoboam, the natural heir to the throne, found himself the villain of the piece as the situation developed. He asked for time—three days—to consider Jeroboam's philosophy. He sought counsel with Solomon's aged advisors, and they all felt that Rehoboam ought to agree to Jeroboam's policies and allow time for consolidation of the nation. At the same time, a more radical group of

Rehoboam's younger counselors recommended that he assert himself immediately. They advised him to answer the people, "My little finger shall be thicker than my father's loins" (I Kings 12:10), meaning that Rehoboam's labor requirements would be even harsher than Solomon's.

When the three days had passed, Rehoboam was completely reckless:

> And the king answered the people roughly, and forsook the old men's counsel that they gave him;

> And spake to them after the counsel of the young men, saying, My father made your yoke heavy, and I will add to your yoke: my father also chastised you with whips, but I will chastise you with scorpions. (I Kings 12:13–14)

This was the blow that divided Israel. Not preferring to be chastised with whips, scorpions, or anything else, the ten northern tribes bolted. They took Jeroboam as their King, and the stubborn Rehoboam ruled over only the Tribes of Judah and Benjamin in the south. Ahijah's prophecy had come out to the letter, so far.

The Hebrew nation would henceforth and for centuries be now referred to as Israel and Judah, in the north and south, respectively.

THE NORTHERN APOSTASY

Once established as King in the north, Jeroboam was not quite the breath of fresh air his subjects may have anticipated. Truly, it was he who had divided the nation, and now he set about being certain it would never reunite.

Jerusalem in the south had a powerful attraction for all of the Hebrew people, of course, and that was the Temple of God. The northern King's private thoughts are revealed in the record:

> And Jeroboam said in his heart, Now shall the kingdom return to the house of David:

> If this people go up to do sacrifice in the house of the Lord at Jerusalem, then shall the heart of this people turn again unto

their lord, even unto Rehoboam king of Judah, and they shall kill me, and go again to Rehoboam king of Judah. (I Kings 12:26–27)

Regardless of Jeroboam's fears, however, the Law was the Law. According to the Law of Moses, which was still being kept to some degree after five centuries, every male Israelite was to worship the Lord at the designated Temple of God during three periods each year. Obviously, there were many sincere northern subjects who wished to keep their faith intact; they would certainly continue their required pilgrimages to the Holy Place.

The cynical Jeroboam placed personal politics above religious faith altogether. His solution to the Temple dilemma was a level of apostasy never seen before among the Chosen People. He created two golden calves—the very sin of Sinai—and claimed that these were the gods that had brought the Hebrew nation out of Egypt. He placed them at pagan altars on the northern and southern extremes of his kingdom, Dan and Bethel. The latter, the Holy Place of Abraham, was thus defiled. There were apparently enough northern apostates willing to follow their new King to create an entirely new order of worship. Jeroboam staffed his heretical sites with a non-Levite priesthood and set up a new schedule of holy convocations.

To read through the intricate particulars of God's laws concerning the exactitude of the holy convocations (Lev. 23), and the precise pattern of the House of Worship (Ex. 25–30), is to appreciate fully the awesome apostasy of Jereboam. The Chosen People had somehow selected an unbelieving King. Jeroboam's worship barely differed from that of the pagan nations across the borders.

The Lord sent an unnamed, but faithful, prophet from Judah, who condemned Jeroboam and his altar at Bethel. The prophet denounced the false worship and declared that a Davidic King named Josiah would ultimately destroy it all. The altar collapsed at a word from this powerful prophet, and when Jeroboam pointed at him to have him arrested, the King's hand withered. The conversation of the King of Israel and the fearless Judean prophet is instructive. We find Jeroboam panicky about his withered hand, pleading with the prophet to entreat God, not some pagan idol, on his behalf:

And the king answered and said unto the man of God, Intreat now the face of the Lord thy God, and pray for me, that my hand may be restored me again. And the man of God besought the Lord, and the king's hand was restored him again, and became as it was before.

And the king said unto the man of God, Come home with me, and refresh thyself, and I will give thee a reward.

And the man of God said unto the king, If thou wilt give me half thine house, I will not go in with thee, neither will I eat bread nor drink water in this place. (I Kings 13:6-8)

And the prophet, shaking the dust off his feet, left the stunned King of Israel standing by his broken altar, thankful only that his extremities were whole again. It is unlikely that Jeroboam ever pointed at another prophet of God.

Nevertheless, Jeroboam continued in apostasy, worshipping as a pagan and appointing the rabble of the land to be priests. His son, Nadab, succeeded him, but was assassinated shortly by a usurper, who then killed all other heirs of Jeroboam.

While the line of David continued unbroken over Judah, the northern throne saw one pagan dynasty after another.

AHAB, JEZEBEL, AND ELIJAH

Three very dramatic characters now enter the chronicles of Israel. Ahab became King in the north about 870 B.C., and the Scriptures devote more space to his reign than that of any other King during the divided kingdom. This is perhaps due to his associations with the prophet Elijah, one of God's truly devout men.

Ahab was an evil man, rebellious against the Lord, and thoroughly idolatrous (I Kings 16:32-33). He would have fitful lapses into repentance and godly obedience, but he was utterly dominated by the degenerate ways of the infamous Jezebel, his wife.

Crafty Jezebel, the daughter of the Phoenician King of Sidon, set about on a one-woman anti-crusade; she made worship of Baal the religion of the land and set up a strong and corrupt priesthood.

Her determined paganism spread through Israel like a disease.

Jezebel delighted in writing letters on behalf of her husband, forging his name and sealing them with his royal seal. She was an expert assassin. She is given due credit in the Scriptures:

> But there was none like unto Ahab, which did sell himself to work wickedness in the sight of the Lord, whom Jezebel his wife stirred up. (I Kings 21:25)

Ahab couldn't begin to handle his wife, and even Elijah was afraid of her (I Kings 19:2–3). Jezebel was the implacable enemy of Elijah, sworn to kill the faithful prophet.

Elijah, the righteous one, became very depressed over the situation in Israel. He fled from Jezebel and the disgusting idolatry to Beersheba, in Judah, and from there to a lonely cave on Mount Horeb, where Moses had received the law. As he sat stricken in the cave, God asked him, "What doest thou here, Elijah?"

> And he said, I have been very jealous for the Lord God of hosts: for the children of Israel have forsaken thy covenant, thrown down thine altars, and slain thy prophets with the sword; and I, even I only, am left; and they seek my life, to take it away. (I Kings 19:10)

How sad. The prophet of God cries out, in effect, "I am the only believer left, and now they are coming for me." God, however, specified that things were not quite that far gone:

> Yet I have left me seven thousand in Israel, all the knees which have not bowed unto Baal, and every mouth which hath not kissed him. (I Kings 19:18).

Ahab, in the meanwhile, made himself comfortable at Samaria, the new northern capital, a well-fortified hill some forty miles north of Jerusalem. There, in opposition to the Spartan principles conveniently espoused by Jeroboam at the time of his selection by the northern tribes, he dwelt in an ivory-covered palace (I Kings 22:38). He also constructed a great altar to Baal, with Jezebel's blessings, and made it the center of worship for the northern kingdom.

Elijah was tireless in his condemnation of Ahab and his odious Phoenician wife. The relationship between the prophet and the King is well expressed in a single verse:

And Ahab said to Elijah, Hast thou found me, O mine enemy? And he answered, I have found thee: because thou hast sold thyself to work evil in the sight of the Lord. (I Kings 21:20)

We will look at the further exploits of the remarkable Elijah in the following chapter.

WAR WITH SYRIA

King Ben-hadad of Damascus was one who appreciated the wealth of Samaria, and brought a huge army to besiege the City. He demanded rights to enter, inspect, and confiscate whatever he wished, but Ahab rejected the terms. For once, the King of Israel consulted with a godly prophet and received the information that he would enjoy victory. Thus, greatly outnumbered, the surprisingly courageous Ahab charged the Syrians with seven thousand soldiers, against the combined army of thirty-two foreign kings (I Kings 19:10; 20:15, 16).

The Syrians retreated to lick their wounds and wonder over the unexpected strength of the northern kingdom of the Hebrews. The matter was spiritual, reasoned Ben-hadad's advisors, and they persuaded him that he could successfully assault Israel again in the valleys. Israel's gods were mountain gods, they said (I Kings 20:23).

But the second invasion was no more successful than the first. The Lord's prophet again assured Ahab of victory (I Kings 20:27–28), though Ahab's forces were again greatly outgunned. Israel's God was found to be effective in the valleys, and Ahab, in a good mood, spared Ben-hadad, a kindness which he lived to regret.

Ahab now turned his attention to beautifying his secondary palace in Jezreel. He chose to have a vineyard to enjoy, next to the palace, but the vineyard happened to belong to a subject named Naboth. Ahab offered to trade Naboth another vineyard for his property, or to buy it, but Naboth refused. It seemed the vineyard was his tribal-family inheritance, and the Law of Moses forbade the selling of such property (Lev. 25:23–24).

The infuriated King, disrespectful as he was of the Law, retired to his bedroom in his Samarian palace and sulked. Increasingly petulant, he even went on a hunger strike. Petty as he was, Ahab did not quite have the gumption to force Naboth to relinquish the vineyard (I Kings 21:1–4).

But his dear wife did. Delighted with the chance for some first-class palace intrigue, Jezebel fed Ahab some soup and put him to bed. Then she sent letters to the corrupt mayor and city council of Jezreel, casually imprinting them with the seal of the King of Israel. She instructed the distant officials to call a public meeting, have Naboth accused of blasphemy by false witnesses, and stoned to death.

The instructions were followed to the letter, and Ahab recovered from his tantrum. The vineyard was his.

Elijah, unable to hold his peace, then returned to confront Ahab about the Lord's disastrous judgment on those who would murder the faithful. Jezebel was to die a violent death, and the dynasty of Ahab would be annihilated (I Kings 21:17–24), he prophesied.

This time, the unpredictable Ahab humbly and sincerely repented, and the Lord was pleased enough with his humility that He said through Elijah that the punishment would await Ahab's death (I Kings 21:27–29).

Three years passed, of relative peace, as Syria regrouped and consolidated a certain amount of captured territory. Then, in a rare display of cooperation between Judah and Israel, King Jehoshaphat offered to join King Ahab in mounting a counterattack against the Syrians to regain remote Gilead.

Jehoshaphat of Judah was well informed of the apostasy of the north, and he requested of his host in the Samarian palace that they consult a prophet from the Lord to advise them concerning the attack. Ahab was more than happy to accommodate him, and produced a heroic array of seers and wizards—some four hundred prophets in all, who were deeply involved with Baal. The four hundred yes-men predicted victory for the united kingdoms.

A bit skeptical, Jehoshaphat asked emphatically, "Is there not here a prophet of the *Lord* besides, that we might enquire of *him*?" (I Kings 22:7).

Ahab has connections, of course, and is able to come up with a true prophet of the Lord, but is loath to do so:

> And the king of Israel said unto Jehoshaphat, There is yet one man, Micaiah the son of Imlah, by whom we may enquire of the Lord: but I hate him; for he doth not prophesy good concerning me, but evil. (I Kings 22:8)

Ahab obviously preferred prophets who understood the preferences of the King around the royal palace. As long as he was about to embark on a military campaign, he might as well have some good news from his reliable soothsayers. It seems not to have occurred to Ahab at all that the prophecies had any meanings, and the prophets of Baal were well aware of how to cultivate their master.

As a matter of fact, they took Micaiah aside, when he was brought in, and gave him strict instructions on how to prophesy. They informed him that they had given a favorable prediction, and that he should certainly follow suit. The King liked to hear of a happy future, they advised Micaiah.

But Micaiah, through whom God Himself spoke, was not going to participate in the fix:

> And Micaiah said, As the Lord liveth, what the Lord saith unto me, that will I speak. (I Kings 22:14)

Micaiah was not one to be trifled with; he angered the King with his predictions:

> And he said, I saw all Israel scattered upon the hills, as sheep that have not a shepherd: and the Lord said, These have no master: let them return every man to his house in peace. (I Kings 22:17)

Deaf to the Word of the Lord, Ahab just wouldn't have it:

> And the king of Israel said unto Jehoshaphat, Did I not tell thee that he would prophesy no good concerning me, but evil? (I Kings 22:18)

The remarkable throne room scene ended in near violence:

And the king of Israel said, Take Micaiah, and carry him back unto Amon the governor of the city, and to Joash the King's son;

And say, Thus saith the king, Put this fellow in the prison, and feed him with bread of affliction and with water of affliction, until I come in peace.

And Micaiah said, If thou return at all in peace, the Lord hath not spoken by me. And he said, Hearken, O people, every one of you. (I Kings 22:26–28)

They should have listened to the prophet. The attack was a disaster. Ahab, and Jehoshaphat with him, went forward mounted for battle, but the King of Israel, steadily losing confidence, took the precaution of disguising himself. Did he possibly believe the annoying Micaiah, after all? In any case, he stripped himself of his royal insignia and went into battle as a simple soldier, while Jehoshaphat retained his regal paraphernalia.

Meanwhile, over in the Syrian camp, the ingrate Ben-hadad instructed special troops to single out King Ahab and kill him on the battlefield. Confused by the royal insignia, the commandos went first for King Jehoshaphat, but when they discovered he was not Ahab they left him alone. Had Ahab's disguise circumvented the prophecy? Had the King of Israel fooled God?

Hardly! By coincidence, a Syrian archer let fly an arrow, without aiming, during the heat of the battle. It found its mark between the joints of Ahab's armor. His aides pulled him away from the conflict, but he died shortly after.

Israel and Judah were completely routed by the Syrians on this occasion, and retreated in humiliation. Ahab was laid to rest at Samaria.

Ahab's long and troubled career had brought nothing but grief to the northern tribes, and his ignominious death spoke clearly of God's wrath upon the idolaters. But the Almighty wasn't finished with them yet. He now took extremely stern measures to cleanse the land of Israel.

GOD'S EXECUTIONER

Jehu, one of Ahab's generals, might be called the Anointed Executioner. Utterly out of patience with Israel's idolatry, God sent Jehu to cleanse with the sword the land which would not heed the prophets.

The divine hatchet man was tireless. He became King by executing Ahab's grandson, Jehoram, and virtually everyone who had ever been seen speaking to him. It was not really a usurpation of royal authority, however, since Jehu was anointed by the prophet Elijah to become the King of Israel (II Kings 9:1–13).

The faithful Elijah had prophesied that Ahab's descendants would not survive, and now the Lord commissioned the fearsome Jehu to guarantee the prophecy. All of Ahab's descendants were to be slain, all of his court, and most especially the wicked Jezebel (II Kings 9:8).

Jehu went about his bloody work with relish. He drove his chariot "furiously," from Ramoth down to Jezreel (II Kings 9:20), and slew Jehoram in the very vineyard of the old martyr Naboth. Jehoram had asked if he came in peace, and Jehu replied that there could be no peace as long as Jezebel conducted her idolatries in the land of Israel. After assassinating Jehoram, he sent a detachment of men to also kill King Ahaziah of Judah, who had been with Jehoram in Jezreel.

Then, Jehu set off on one of his very difficult assignments: the assassination of Jezebel. The wily ex-queen, dangerous as a tarantula even in her old age, put on her makeup ("painted her face"), costumed herself beautifully, and looked down out of a high window on Jehu and his chariot. She inquired of Jehu if Zimri had enjoyed any peace when he killed King Elah years ago (Zimri, in fact, had gone to his grave a suicide, seven days after he assassinated Elah; I Kings 16:9–10). Jezebel still had an idea or two on how to get under a man's skin.

Jehu ignored her question and its implications, and, instead, asked the eunuchs who attended her if they were on his side. If they were, he said, they could oblige him by tossing the old witch out of her window.

And he said, Throw her down. So they threw her down: and some of her blood was sprinkled on the wall, and on the horses: and he trode her under foot. (II Kings 9:33)

Jehu then calmly entered the building and sat down to supper. Thinking over the situation after dessert, he told his lieutenants to go out and bury Jezebel's body, since she was, after all, the daughter of a King (the King of Sidon).

But the record relates:

And they went to bury her: but they found no more of her than the skull, and the feet, and the palms of her hands.

Wherefore they came again, and told him. And he said, This is the word of the Lord, which he spake by his servant Elijah the Tishbite, saying, In the portion of Jezreel shall dogs eat the flesh of Jezebel:

And the carcase of Jezebel shall be as dung upon the face of the field in the portion of Jezreel; so that they shall not say, This is Jezebel. (II Kings 9:35–37)

Jezebel may have been Jehu's trophy when it came to cleansing Israel, but he was really only warming to his task. He next turned to the sons of Joram, in order to literally wipe out all the descendants of Ahab. But here he found a monumental task. The prolific Joram and his Solomonic collection of wives had begotten seventy sons, and Jehu was kept extremely busy. God's assassin finally did track down all seventy heirs of the former royal line; and then he began on the priests of Baal.

There were a lot of priests of Baal in Israel, as we can well imagine. Ahab could produce four hundred prophets at the palace with a snap of the royal finger. But, at length, the thorough one finished them all off.

Curiously, all the killing that Jehu did was in obedience to the Lord, and he was one of Israel's most obedient Kings. However, he seemed to miss the full point of his own assignment. After the land had been cleansed of the idolatrous priests, and the pagan line of heirs to the throne, Jehu established his reign—but he kept those golden calves at Dan and Bethel. Israel continued to worship gods of gold, rather than Baal in person, but they utterly failed to return to the Lord. And they also failed to return to Jerusalem.

The assassin ruled the northern kingdom for twenty-eight years, died in bed, and was buried in Samaria.

THE FALL OF ISRAEL

The northern kingdom staggered on, with one false dynasty after another, usurping and reusurping the throne. Wars of succession came and went, while the Kingdom of Israel continued in idolatry and every sort of evil. Judah, in the south, remained intact; at least, so far as the royal dynasty was concerned. The descendants of King David continued to rule in the Holy City, as God had prophesied. The Davidic dynasty was to remain in force forever.

God sent Israel incomparable prophets, but they were not able to effect a lasting change in the Kings or the people. The Scriptural record becomes a litany; each King "did that which was evil in the sight of the Lord."

Finally, inevitably, the patience of Jehovah was exhausted. In 721 B.C., Shalmaneser, the King of Assyria, invaded and captured Israel and its capital, Samaria. Hoshea was the King at that time, and he became the servant of Shalmaneser. The ten tribes were taken away from the land and resettled in various provinces of Assyria in captivity—these are the "ten lost tribes" but the likelihood is that they were not lost at all. The Hebrew people were later restored to Israel, as we shall see, and the Book of James, in the New Testament, is addressed "To the Twelve Tribes" (James 1:1).

The people of Israel had terribly hard times among the Assyrians. Their captors were one of the most cruel and sadistic peoples of antiquity. They slaughtered thousands, and moved whole populations about where it best benefited their own plans and resources. But God takes quite a lengthy passage to explain this extraordinary punishment (II Kings 17:3–23). The Lord enumerates with perfect accuracy the long list of sins "that the children of Israel had sinned against the Lord their God, which had brought them up out of the land of Egypt, from under the hand of Pharaoh king of Egypt, and had feared other gods, And walked in the statutes of the heathen, whom the Lord cast out from before the children of Israel, and of the kings of Israel, which they had made" (II Kings 17:7–8).

Idolatry is the theme of the passage:

For they served idols, whereof the Lord had said unto them, Ye shall not do this thing.

REVIVAL IN JUDAH

While Israel was on the verge of being carried off, Judah was enjoying its greatest surge of spiritual renewal in its history. The righteous Hezekiah had succeeded to the throne. He received more praise for faithfulness than any other Hebrew King:

And he did that which was right in the sight of the Lord, according to all that David his father did.

He removed the high places, and brake the images, and cut down the groves, and brake in pieces the brasen serpent that Moses had made: for unto those days the children of Israel did burn incense to it: and he called it Nehushtan.

He trusted in the Lord God of Israel; so that after him was none like him among all the kings of Judah, nor any that were before him.

For he clave to the Lord, and departed not from following him, but kept his commandments, which the Lord commanded Moses. (II Kings 18:3–6)

In his zeal for the Lord, Hezekiah made it his personal business to tear down all the many temples and altars that had been built to pagan gods during the three hundred years of the preceding monarchy. The people had even been worshipping Moses' brass serpent (Num. 21:5–9), which was, by then, a seven-hundred-year-old relic. Hezekiah destroyed it, rather than see it continue to be a totem.

Hezekiah left only the Holy Temple of God in Jerusalem for worship, and that was exactly his intention. Judah was now, of course, a very small and weak province, only a fraction of what the entire Hebrew nation had been. Some ten years after Shalmaneser had taken Israel captive, his successor, Sennacherib, attacked Judah and captured a number of the cities. Hezekiah was forced to pay taxes to Assyria, in return for their retreat, and thus Jerusalem was spared. Enormous sums of money which drained the national treasury were paid in tribute to Assyria, but, at least, God's city was secure.

But the predatory Sennacherib was still not satisfied. Despite the enormous taxes, he wanted Jerusalem itself. He sent a special officer called "The Rabshakeh" to intimidate Hezekiah and Jerusalem. The Rabshakeh was a master of propaganda, and camped with a delegation outside the city to taunt the Hebrew people.

Meanwhile, Hezekiah fortified Jerusalem and built a remarkable tunnel bringing water from the springs into the walled city, draining all of the springs around the walls that might comfort an invader. The King pleaded with the people to trust in the Lord for deliverance:

Be strong and courageous, be not afraid nor dismayed for the king of Assyria, nor for all the multitude that is with him: for there be more with us than with him:

With him is an arm of flesh; but with us is the Lord our God to help us, and to fight our battles. And the people rested themselves upon the words of Hezekiah king of Judah. (II Chron. 32:7–8)

The Rabshakeh and his delegation needled the people of Jerusalem constantly. The demoralizing Rabshakeh spoke good Hebrew and informed the population of Jerusalem that they were foolish to trust in their Lord God, because none of the other gods of any other country had ever been able to ward off the Assyrians.

The insolence continued without reaction from the Jews:

But the people held their peace, and answered him not a word: for the king's commandment was, saying, Answer him not. (II Kings 18:36)

Actually, one Eliakim had gone out to Rabshakeh and told him, "Speak, I pray thee, to thy servants in the Syrian language; for we understand it," which had a quality of irony the Rabshakeh could appreciate.

In truth, Hezekiah was very frightened and in anguish. From what he could see, Jerusalem didn't stand a chance. Between Assyria's public relations machine and their virtually invincible army, the enemy was simply overwhelming. But Hezekiah went to the Temple and prayed, and asked the Lord to deliver Jerusalem.

Isaiah, one of the Lord's great men, came forward and reported to Hezekiah that God would answer his prayer. The Assyrian army would be struck with a plague and King Sennacherib would be assassinated back in his homeland.

With complete confidence, Hezekiah told the Rabshakeh that Jerusalem would continue to rely on the Lord. With that, the Rabshakeh's mission was over and he reported to Sennacherib that the King of Jerusalem was immovable. Sennacherib took the trouble to send a letter to Hezekiah, warning him that the Lord could not possibly save Jerusalem from his armies. Hezekiah took the letter with him to the Temple and prayed again for deliverance, and Isaiah again came forward with a repeat performance: the answer was still the same; the Lord would protect Jerusalem from the Assyrians.

That very night, the Angel of the Lord smote the encamped army of Assyria with an awesome plague that left 185,000 troops dead, including all officers. The astounded King Sennacherib retreated in shame to his capital, Nineveh, where he was later assassinated by his own sons.

Sometime later, Hezekiah became gravely ill, and Isaiah counseled him that he should get ready to die. But the faithful one prayed once more; this time, that the Lord would spare his own life. The dependable Isaiah returned with the answer, as usual, saying that the Lord would give Hezekiah fifteen more years, and would continue to protect Jerusalem from Assyria. Isaiah instructed the King's servants in a certain medical treatment—a fig compress—and the mortally stricken Hezekiah responded well. The King asked God for a sign that he would indeed recover, and the Lord turned back the shadow on the sundial ten degrees before the appreciative Hezekiah.

The conversation accompanying this stupefying miracle illustrates the patience of God with a good servant:

And Isaiah said, This sign shalt thou have of the Lord, that the Lord will do the thing that he hath spoken: shall the shadow go forward ten degrees, or go back ten degrees?

And Hezekiah answered, It is a light thing for the shadow to go down ten degrees: nay, but let the shadow return backward ten degrees.

And Isaiah the prophet cried unto the Lord: and he brought the shadow ten degrees backward, by which it had gone down in the dial of Ahaz. (II Kings 20: 9–11)

God had moved the world for Hezekiah.

Unfortunately, like his ancestor Moses, Hezekiah fell into one serious sin. The friendly King of Babylon had sent a get-well present to the King of Judah, and Hezekiah took the opportunity to show the Babylonian messengers all the treasuries and armaments of Judah. He had forgotten that the treasuries and armaments of Judah had seemed far too little during the siege of Jerusalem, and that God, alone, had saved the city.

Isaiah was most displeased with this sin of pride, and prophesied to Hezekiah that one day all the treasury of Judah would be hauled off to Babylon, and the King's own descendants would be made eunuchs in the palace of the King of Babylon. The prophecy, as it happened, was fulfilled within a century.

Hezekiah lived his fifteen more allotted years, and died in peace around 687 B.C.

THE LOST BIBLE

Hezekiah's young son, Manasseh, learned nothing from his father and ruled for an unfortunately long time:

Manasseh was twelve years old when he began to reign, and reigned fifty and five years in Jerusalem. And his mother's name was Hephzibah.

And he did that which was evil in the sight of the Lord, after the abominations of the heathen, whom the Lord cast out before the children of Israel.

For he built up again the high places which Hezekiah his father had destroyed; and he reared up altars for Baal, and made a grove, as did Ahab king of Israel; and worshipped all the host of heaven [the stars and planets, as in astrology], and served them. (II Kings 21:1–3)

The paganism got so bad in Judah that the Lord compared it to the Canaanite nations, who had occupied the land at the time of Joshua:

But they hearkened not: and Manasseh seduced them to do more evil than did the nations whom the Lord destroyed before the children of Israel. (II Kings 21:9)

God was infuriated:

And the Lord spake by his servants the prophets, saying,

Because Manasseh king of Judah hath done these abominations, and hath done wickedly above all that the Amorites did, which were before him, and hath made Judah also to sin with his idols:

Therefore thus saith the Lord God of Israel, Behold, I am bringing such evil upon Jerusalem and Judah, that whosoever heareth of it, both his ears shall tingle. (II Kings 21:10–12)

Manasseh's son, Amon, succeeded him on the throne, but was hardly an improvement. This time Jehovah had little patience. Amon was assassinated by his own servants after a reign of two years. Judah was obviously headed in the direction of irreverent Israel before it.

But then came the upright Josiah, whose name means "The Lord saves." He took the throne as an eight-year-old, around 650 B.C., and before his brief lifetime was over, he nearly restored the entire Hebrew nation to their true God.

The Temple of God, now a three-hundred-year-old structure, had fallen into disrepair, and Josiah set out to restore it to its former perfection. In the report about the course of the work, a peculiar verse occurs in the record:

And Hilkiah the high priest said unto Shaphan the scribe, I have found the book of the law in the house of the Lord. And Hilkiah gave the book to Shaphan, and he read it. (II Kings 22:8)

Remarkable! The "Book of the Law" had been lost and now was found! The passage probably refers to the Torah, or at least the definitive Book of Deuteronomy. In any case, the Law of the land had been discarded so long before that it was now discovered only by workmen who sought to repair breaks in the sanctuary wall. The verse also may indicate that the high priest could not read; he called in a scribe in order to find out what the book said.

It is overwhelming to consider the enormity of this disclosure. That extremely detailed and complex Law that God had personally presented to Moses at Sinai had been all but forgotten, and the high priest of the land was previously not even aware of it!

Shaphan the scribe thought to take the interesting old book to the King. He had discovered a relic, after all. He may have been surprised by Josiah's response:

And it came to pass, when the king had heard the words of the book of the law, that he rent his clothes. (II Kings 22:11)

The youthful Josiah, now twenty-six years old, had a more penetrating appreciation of the Law of Moses than did anyone else in Judah, it seems:

Go ye, enquire of the Lord for me, and for the people, and for all Judah, concerning the words of this book that is found: for great is the wrath of the Lord that is kindled against us, because our fathers have not hearkened unto the words of this book, to do according unto all that which is written concerning us. (II Kings 22:13)

The prophetess Huldah gave a dire prediction. Judah had sinned so gravely that the Lord's judgment on Jerusalem was inevitable. But since Josiah was repentant when he became acquainted with the Book of the Law, God would grant him this: He would die before the judgment.

Josiah immediately began extensive reforms in his kingdom that made him one of the most feared, but respected, Kings in the history of the Hebrew people. First, he decided that every subject of his should hear the words of the Law, and he read it all to them:

And the king sent, and they gathered unto him all the elders of Judah and of Jerusalem.

And the king went up into the house of the Lord, and all the men of Judah and all the inhabitants of Jerusalem with him, and the priests, and the prophets, and all the people, both small and great: and he read in their ears all the words of the book of the covenant which was found in the house of the Lord. (II Kings 23:1-2)

Josiah rallied the people in a fervent covenant made before the Lord:

And the king stood by a pillar, and made a covenant before the Lord, to walk after the Lord, and to keep his commandments and his testimonies and his statutes with all their heart and all their soul, to perform the words of this covenant that were written in this book. And all the people stood to the covenant. (II Kings 23:3)

The reforms began right at the Temple, where Josiah tore out all the pagan altars and stopped the idolatry:

And he brought out the grove from the house of the Lord, without Jerusalem, unto the brook Kidron, and burned it at the brook Kidron, and stamped it small to powder, and cast the powder thereof upon the graves of the children of the people. (II Kings 23:6)

He then continued throughout the land of Judah and even into Israel, like a tornado, breaking down "holy" places to the pagan gods, digging up the graves of former idolaters, and truly cleansing the Promised Land. The idol worshippers fell back in awe when King Josiah came through town.

He did not omit the former Kingdom of Israel—traveling to the altar that was at Bethel and smashing it. He killed all the pagan priests and purposely burned their bones on their own altars, a sure way to pollute a pagan altar.

When this painful process was finished, Josiah ordered that there be a national observance of Passover. Probably, there had been some private observances of the Passover throughout the history of the Hebrews, but the King set up a border-to-border, town-by-town universal commemoration of the deliverance of the Chosen People. Such a celebration had not been seen since the time of Joshua, over seven centuries. The Almighty had a very high opinion of this Passover:

Surely there was not holden such a passover from the days of the judges that judged Israel, nor in all the days of the kings of Israel, nor of the kings of Judah;

But in the eighteenth year of king Josiah, wherein this passover was holden to the Lord in Jerusalem. (II Kings 23:22–23)

In 608 B.C., when Josiah was thirty-nine years old, Pharaoh Nechoh of Egypt, crossed Israel with his army on his way to Assyria. The battle was between Egypt and Assyria, but Josiah didn't like the idea of the trespassing. He went out personally with an army to intercept Pharaoh (II Chron. 35:20–21).

Pharaoh had no quarrel with Josiah, but he sent a very strange message: He told the King of Judah not to interfere with the progress of his army because it was God's Will that he attack Assyria. Josiah's own perception of God's Will was quite different, of course.

It all ended with Josiah trying to stop the huge Egyptian army.

A stray arrow found the godly King and felled him in the field. He was carried back to Jerusalem mortally wounded, and he succumbed in the Holy City. All Judah mourned his death, and two centuries later the prophet Zechariah recounts that this was one of the most tragic moments in Israel's history (Zech. 12:11).

True to God's Word on the matter, the young Josiah died before he could see what was to become of his kingdom. God had in mind now the terrible discipline that He had pronounced against Jerusalem and Judah. Nebuchadnezzar of Babylon was poised on the northern border ready to attack. The Hebrew people were about to lose the Temple of God and be taken into captivity in Babylon—a blow from which they would not fully recover until A.D. 1948. This deportation would be the beginning of the end for Israel until the present day—they would not again enjoy autonomy over their own land until the twentieth century!

The righteous Josiah's reforms were complete and more than sincere, but they were a last-gasp effort that could not stem the tide. Jehovah had decided. There had just been too much idolatry, too many uncaring Kings, and too much living outside the law of Moses. The Chosen People were now to be severely disciplined.

We turn now to the prophets, and then to one of the saddest chapters in the history of ancient Israel—the terrorism of the vicious Nebuchadnezzar, one of the most savage conquerors in all antiquity.

9

"Thus Saith the Lord": The Grand Age of the Prophets

They were the voice of God to His people. They introduced themselves with perfect confidence: "Thus saith the Lord."

Their predictions were not confined to Old Testament times, New Testament times, or even modern times; much Old Testament prophecy is tied to future ages and yet to be fulfilled. They enjoyed, through the workings of God, an amazing view of history. They saw, in effect, all things happening at once. The accuracy of Old Testament prophecy has been verified throughout the story of mankind, and the veracity of the Bible, if it rested on nothing else, can be fully appreciated through the sayings of the prophets.

They came into being when the monarchy was established. Earlier, during the times of the Judges, the Judges themselves served as prophets of the Lord, but now a special office was created and the voice of the Lord came to the King and the people through this variety of faithful men. They were the inspired conscience of the nation.

They came of all kinds. Some were noblemen in the courts of Kings; others were priests; still others were farmers, herdsmen, and plain, humble working folk; but they all spoke the same basic message: "Return to the Lord and His law, beware His judgment, and, above all things, look for the glorious future day of Messiah."

THE FIRST WRITING PROPHET

The last of the Judges was the first writing prophet of Israel. Samuel, who shepherded Israel through the transition from rule by Judges to rule by Kings, was, in effect, the first official prophet.

His birth was an answer to prayer. His mother Hannah was barren, and she prayed with her husband Elkanah at the Tabernacle at Shiloh for a child. She promised she would dedicate her child to the Lord. The priest Eli saw her praying and petitioned the Lord to grant her wish. Samuel was born within the year, and true to her word, Hannah took the child, at the age of weaning, to Eli, to dedicate him to the service of the Lord. Thus, Samuel was brought up by Eli in the House of God. Showing unmistakable approval, the Almighty blessed Elkanah and Hannah with five more children after Samuel.

Samuel actually lived at Shiloh with Eli, and when he was awakened by someone calling his name one night, he assumed it was the priest. Three times the youngster's sleep was disturbed, and each time he faithfully reported to the bewildered Eli. Finally, it became clear that it was God Himself who was calling young Samuel.

The first message the Lord gave to Samuel was a hard one to deliver. There was to be a judgment against his foster father, Eli because of the embezzlement his sons were conducting out of the offerings at the Tabernacle. But the child prophet spoke the words of the Lord to Eli, and the priest sighed with resignation: "It is the Lord: let him do what seemeth him good" (I Sam. 3:18).

Through this prophecy and several others that followed, Samuel's fame spread throughout Israel.

After the prophet had become a Judge, he wished his sons to succeed him, but they were no improvement on Eli's sons. The sons of Samuel took bribes and had little respect for the justice their own father administered. The people rejected the idea of further Judges, in any case. They wanted to have a King, like the other nations had (I Sam. 8:5–7).

Samuel didn't take to the idea of the people having a King, feeling that it was a personal rejection of himself and his heirs. God, however, stated that it was the Almighty whom the people were rejecting, not Samuel. God had promised Israel a King indeed, back in the time of Abraham. But He was most disappointed in the people's motive. It seemed to be out of admiration of the other nations that Israel chose to be a monarchy.

But God did give them a King: Saul, of the Tribe of Benjamin, who was "head and shoulders" taller than most men of Israel (though he shrank from taking on Goliath, as we have seen), was selected and anointed by Samuel. The prophet charged him to rule Israel in utter obedience to the Lord (I Sam. 10:1, 24).

One of the hazards of being a prophet were those hard days when one had to rebuke a King. Certainly, the Kings themselves got out of line, and King Saul was no exception. During a battle with the Amalekites, Saul failed to fulfill the complete instructions of the Lord (to kill all of them). Saul saved some of the animals to sacrifice them to God, and also spared the life of the Amalekite King Agag. Samuel stepped forward with an explicit sermon on the theme that God wanted obedience rather than sacrifice. Samuel taught:

Hath the Lord as great delight in burnt offerings and sacrifices, as in obeying the voice of the Lord? Behold, to obey is better than sacrifice, and to hearken than the fat of rams.

For rebellion is as the sin of witchcraft, and stubbornness is as iniquity and idolatry. Because thou hast rejected the word of the Lord, he hath also rejected thee from being king. (I Sam. 15:22–23)

The King had a repentant attitude, but it was too late for repentance:

And Saul said unto Samuel, I have sinned: for I have transgressed the commandment of the Lord, and thy words: because I feared the people, and obeyed their voice.

Now therefore, I pray thee, pardon my sin, and turn again with me, that I may worship the Lord.

And Samuel said unto Saul, I will not return with thee: for thou hast rejected the word of the Lord, and the Lord hath rejected thee from being king over Israel. (I Sam. 15:24–26)

Samuel then dealt with the Amalekite King personally:

Then said Samuel, Bring ye hither to me Agag the king of the Amalekites. And Agag came unto him delicately. And Agag said, Surely the bitterness of death is past.

And Samuel said, As thy sword hath made women childless, so shall thy mother be childless among women. And Samuel hewed Agag in pieces before the Lord in Gilgal. (I Sam. 15:32–33)

Truly, Saul's reign saw a decline from that time forward, and the Spirit of God was obviously no longer with him. Samuel went off to anoint the young David as Israel's next King, while Saul's rule deteriorated into a succession of military campaigns along the borders.

We have seen that Samuel's choice of the whimsical young David was rather unique. Indeed, David hailed from the designated royal Tribe of Judah in the family of Jesse, but was, of course, the least likely choice of Jesse's sons. Samuel's reasoning is among the central pillars of Biblical truth: "Man looketh on the outward appearance, but the Lord looketh on the heart" (I Sam. 16:7).

Samuel continued to prophesy during David's early years, but died before the death of Saul.

That was not the end of Samuel's ministry, however; he returned from the grave to consult with King Saul!

It's certainly one of the stranger moments in Scripture—this instance when a prophet returned from the dead. It seemed that Saul was concerned about a certain battle against the Philistines, and instead of seeking out a living prophet, he felt he could trust only the faithful Samuel, who by that time had passed on. The King went to a witch in Endor and asked her to bring back Samuel so that he could consult with him. The Lord allowed this unprecedented combination of faith and heresy—the total belief in the righteous Samuel vs. the violation of the law against sorcery (I Sam. 28:7–20).

Samuel indeed came forth, and his message was harsh. Israel would be defeated by the Philistines the next day, and the King and his sons would be dead and with Samuel. Saul collapsed at this news, but recovered enough to attend the battle.

The next day Saul's sons were all killed on the battlefield and the King committed suicide.

THE PROPHET OF FIRE

The volatile Elijah was the next major prophet to come on the scene, some two centuries after Samuel. His ministry, as we saw in the previous chapter, was to the northern kingdom during the reign of King Ahab. He was the tireless rebuker of the evil works of Ahab and Jezebel, and Ahab gave Elijah his due. He considered the infuriating prophet his greatest nemesis (II Kings 1:8).

Elijah once announced to Ahab that there would be no rain until he, Elijah, said so. And, indeed, no rain fell for three and a half years. There was terrible famine during that time in Israel, though Elijah was fed by wild birds across the Jordan River, and later in the home of a Gentile widow. The widow had only a piece of bread and a little jar of oil when Elijah came to stay with her and her son. The two had planned to finish their bread with the oil and then starve to death together. But when Elijah, the consummate house guest, began his residency, the oil and bread were miraculously replenished every day for all three of them, and they survived the lean years.

While the famine was still on, Elijah challenged Ahab to bring his trusted team of the four hundred priests of Baal to Mount Carmel (near modern Haifa) for a public contest against the Lord. An altar was to be prepared, with the animals and firewood in place, and then Baal and God would be tested at the task of sending fire down to burn the sacrifices. The pagan priests took the challenge and entreated Baal with prayer, shouting, and even mortification of their own flesh; but, unfortunately, no fire ensued. Elijah then stepped forward and dramatically ordered the priests to pour sea water on the altar until it would soak through. He then asked the Lord to show that He was, indeed, the God of Israel. Tremendous fire issued down from heaven, burned up the soaking wet animals and wood, and left the crowd speechless.

The onlookers immediately fell in worship to the true God, and subsequently obeyed Elijah's order to slay the four hundred priests by the now dry River of Kishon, at the base of Mount Carmel.

Now that at least a part of the people had returned to the Lord, Elijah prayed for rain. Three times he sent his assistant to look for a cloud over the blue Mediterranean, and on the third trip he did report a diminutive cloud the "size of a man's hand." The confident Elijah then sent an urgent message to Ahab that he had better get home quickly before he got overtaken by a flash flood. Sure enough, the rains finally came that day. The long drought was over.

Elijah had a much greater fear of Jezebel than of Ahab and his four hundred priests. The man who could turn rain on and off fled in real terror of the dangerous Queen, who had issued his death warrant. It was on that trip, through Beersheba and into the Sinai Desert, that Elijah, in deep depression, complained that he was the only faithful Israelite left. God reassured the depressed one on that occasion (I Kings 19:18).

The Lord now recommissioned Elijah with several important tasks. He was to anoint his own successor, Elisha; to anoint the new King of Syria; and to return to Israel, where he was to anoint Jehu the Assassin as the eventual northern King. God was certainly planning ahead at this point.

Reinvigorated, Elijah made his way back out of the Sinai, and he presently passed the farm of the strong young Elisha. Elisha was busily plowing a field behind twelve oxen, a monumental task. The respected prophet approached him and laid his mantle on Elisha's back.

Elisha was deeply moved by this sanctified gesture:

And he left the oxen, and ran after Elijah, and said, Let me, I pray thee, kiss my father and my mother, and then I will follow thee. And he said unto him, Go back again: for what have I done to thee?

And he returned back from him, and took a yoke of oxen, and slew them, and boiled their flesh with the instruments of the oxen, and gave unto the people, and they did eat. Then he arose, and went after Elijah, and ministered unto him. (I Kings 19:20–21)

The youth Elisha became, in effect, the first prophet-in-training, and he went on as Elijah's personal attendant and protégé.

We covered a large portion of Elijah's ministry in the previous chapter; the continuing events of his opposition to the monarchy of the northern tribes comprised his major assignment. We would now report his death, but we cannot do that since he never died. Elijah was taken directly to heaven, and, so far as we know, is still alive.

It was a complex undertaking, this translation. Elijah was in Gilgal, some twenty-five miles north of Jerusalem, one day, and felt called to make a stop at Bethel, about ten miles south. He bade Elisha to stay where he was, but his apprentice insisted on making the trip. At Bethel, the two were greeted by the "Sons of the Prophets," who were probably men who had studied the past and present prophets of the Lord, somewhat like our seminary students and professors today. These worthies revealed to Elisha something he somehow already knew:

And the sons of the prophets that were at Bethel came forth to Elisha, and said unto him, Knowest thou that the Lord will take away thy master from thy head to day? And he said, Yea, I know it; hold ye your peace. (II Kings 2:3)

Elijah packed up for another journey, informing Elisha that the Lord now wanted the elder prophet to go down into the Jordan Valley to Jericho. Elisha was again ordered to remain at Bethel, but again insisted on accompanying his master. We should appreciate that these were lengthy and arduous trips through arid Judea.

At Jericho, another group of "Sons of the Prophets" met them and the dialogue was virtually repeated.

Then Elijah told his protégé to wait in Jericho while he went down to the Jordan River, and again Elisha said, in effect, "I am already packed. Let's go." This time, the fifty men from the Jericho "seminary" accompanied them and watched at a distance. Elijah hit the water with his coat, and the Jordan divided so the two could cross!

The aged prophet and his eager pupil now held their last conversation there on the east bank of the Jordan:

> And it came to pass, when they were gone over, that Elijah said unto Elisha, Ask what I shall do for thee, before I be taken away from thee. And Elisha said, I pray thee, let a double portion of thy spirit be upon me.

> And he said, Thou hast asked a hard thing: nevertheless, if thou see me when I am taken from thee, it shall be so unto thee; but if not, it shall not be so. (II Kings 2:9–10)

Thus Elisha requested double the prophetic skill of his mentor. The record follows with a scene unparalleled in the entire Bible:

> And it came to pass, as they still went on, and talked, that, behold, there appeared a chariot of fire, and horses of fire, and parted them both asunder; and Elijah went up by a whirlwind into heaven.

> And Elisha saw it, and he cried, My father, my father, the chariot of Israel, and the horsemen thereof. And he saw him no more: and he took hold of his own clothes, and rent them in two pieces. (II Kings 2:11–12)

"DOUBLE THY SPIRIT"

Elisha took up the mantle of the departed Elijah and began his ministry at that very moment. As the stupefied Jericho fifty watched, the youthful prophet smote the Jordan with the mantle in the grand tradition of his master. He cried out, "Where is the Lord God of Elijah?" and the waters obediently parted. The triumphant Elisha crossed the dry riverbed, as the fifty bowed down before him in wonder.

Not accustomed to witnessing such miracles (and who is?), the Jericho group insisted on sending out a search party for the body of Elijah. The Lord had taken him up—that much they had all seen—but perhaps he had then dropped him back in the mountains. Elisha said it was entirely a waste of time but they searched the mountains anyway. Elisha well knew that Elijah was with God in heaven, of course. The search went on without result for three days:

And when they came again to him, (for he tarried at Jericho,) he said unto them, Did I not say unto you, Go not? (II Kings 2:18)

Elisha then performed a further miracle at Jericho, which was very useful to the city. The residents complained that the water there was polluted, and the prophet took some salt, poured it on the city spring, and announced that the Lord had now purified the water.

To this day, Jericho is a lush oasis in a most arid section of the Jordan Valley, providing fresh, clean water for all who pass.

Meanwhile, the military campaigns were continuing as usual. When King Ahab's grandson, Jehoram, ruled Israel, Moab revolted and Jehoram, King Jehoshaphat of Judah, and the King of Edom joined forces to attack. The three Kings devised an ambitious plan; they would circle the southern end of the Dead Sea and sneak up on Moab from its weak, southern border. But after seven days of travel in that barren, thankless desert country, the invaders ran out of water for their horses and cattle.

Jehoshaphat the faithful asked for a prophet of the Lord, as was his lifelong habit. Elisha came along, carping about the presence of the faithless Kings of Israel and Edom:

And Elisha said, As the Lord of hosts liveth, before whom I stand, surely, were it not that I regard the presence of Jehoshaphat the king of Judah, I would not look toward thee, nor see thee. (II Kings 3:14)

The unpredictable young prophet then ordered up a musician:

But now bring me a minstrel. And it came to pass, when the minstrel played, that the hand of the Lord came upon him. (II Kings 3:15)

Thus fortified, Elisha told the three Kings to dig ditches in the dry valley.

Before their collected armies, the three royal ditchdiggers went to work. Shortly, the ditches were miraculously filled with water and the animals were refreshed. Elisha then added to his pronouncement the heartening note:

And this is but a light thing in the sight of the Lord: he will deliver the Moabites also into your hand. (II Kings 3:18)

For their part, the Moabites were quite confident of their southern flank. What army would try to cross those vast desert flats? Their sentries spotted the movements of the combined armies, however, and the Moabites armed a border force to meet them.

Even more unaccustomed to miracles of the Lord than were their neighbors of Jericho, the Moabites then made a serious mistake:

And they rose up early in the morning, and the sun shone upon the water, and the Moabites saw the water on the other side as red as blood:

And they said, This is blood: the kings are surely slain, and they have smitten one another: now therefore, Moab, to the spoil. (II Kings 3:22–23)

The Moabites had spotted the pools of water, but interpreted that they were pools of blood. The crazed and thirsty armies in the desert must have attacked each other, they reckoned, and they sent out their forces for a mop-up operation.

The invaders had gotten up early that morning, too, and, needless to say, that was the end of Moab for a long while.

Elisha continued through the land of Israel, doing miracle after miracle and more than demonstrating that he possessed double the spirit of Elijah. He multiplied a seminary widow's supply of oil so that her two sons would not have to be sold into slavery (II Kings 4:1–7). He did a very big favor for a kindly couple who had provided him a "prophet's chamber" while he traveled in Shunem —he raised their son from the dead (II Kings 4:34). He stopped to make a lost axehead float to the surface of the muddy Jordan

River (II Kings 6:6), and reassured the people of Samaria during a Syrian siege that they would be victorious (II Kings 7:1).

The story of the Syrian general Naaman demonstrated the extension of God's blessings to those outside of Israel. Naaman suffered terribly from leprosy, and desperately sought a cure. He had an Israelite maid in his household, whom he had captured in one of his Israeli campaigns. She informed her master about the miracle worker Elisha in Samaria. Naaman, the sworn enemy of Israel, wrote a letter to the King in Samaria begging an audience with Elisha. The King of Israel was, of course, loath to comfort the enemy general, and thought Naaman was using his disease as an excuse for safe passage right into the royal court. Elisha, however, consulted with the King and told him to let the general come and see for himself that the Lord had a true prophet in Israel.

The ailing general was deeply grateful, but, as he approached Elisha's house, the prophet sent a messenger out to tell him to go down to the Jordan River and simply dip himself seven times—this would cure the leprosy.

The general was insulted. He had come seeking a first-class healing, and he wanted to see a real miracle. He wanted to see Elisha smite things with his mighty hand and call down the great forces of heaven, and here he was merely being sent on what seemed to be a silly errand:

But Naaman was wroth, and went away, and said, Behold, I thought, He will surely come out to me, and stand, and call on the name of the Lord his God, and strike his hand over the place, and recover the leper. (II Kings 5:11)

He even carped about the muddy Jordan. The rivers of Syria, he observed in a huff, were certainly more healthful and wholesome than those of Israel:

Are not Abana and Pharpar, rivers of Damascus, better than all the waters of Israel? May I not wash in them, and be clean? So he turned and went away in a rage. (II Kings 5:12)

Fortunately, the servants of Naaman prevailed upon him with a reasonable argument, and the story has a happy ending:

And his servants came near, and spake unto him, and said, My father, if the prophet had bid thee do some great thing, wouldest thou not have done it? how much rather then, when he saith to thee, Wash, and be clean?

Then went he down, and dipped himself seven times in the Jordan, according to the saying of the man of God: and his flesh came again like unto the flesh of a little child, and he was clean. (II Kings 5:13–14)

Naaman then became a true worshipper of God, understandably:

And he returned to the man of God, he and all his company, and came, and stood before him: and he said, Behold, now I know that there is no God in all the earth, but in Israel; now therefore, I pray thee, take a blessing of thy servant. (II Kings 5:15)

The blessing Naaman wished to bestow was money, but Elisha refused the payment. The prophet's servant, Gehazi, greedily ran after Naaman, however, and asked for a commission of two talents of silver. The grateful general provided these gladly, but when Gehazi returned, Elisha let the punishment fit the crime. Naaman's leprosy was now transferred to the avaricious Gehazi (II Kings 5:26–27).

The remarkable Elisha just slips away in the Scriptural record. Nothing at all is said about his death.

"BEWARE THE DAY OF THE LORD"

A prophet of disaster, Joel continually sounded the alarm. His words to the wise are still in effect. His prophecies reach well beyond our own times.

He was a prophet of extremely "long range." Equally skilled at foretelling the events of ancient Israel, and the events of the coming Kingdom of God on earth, Joel's brief book sweeps over the millennia in breath-taking perspective.

Joel may have known Elijah, and he was certainly a contemporary of Elisha.

The nation experienced a devastating plague of locusts during Joel's time and lost valuable crops. The prophet took this opportunity to warn the people that a much greater plague was coming—an armed invasion which would destroy all of the northern kingdom. Indeed, a century later, the Assyrians carried off the ten tribes and came very close to destroying Judah as well (Joel 1:4; 2:2–4).

If the locusts foreshadowed the Assyrian invasion, then the invasion itself foreshadowed something even more devastating. Joel's term "the Day of the Lord" refers to a time in our own future of great tribulation for Israel and the world, ending in an enormous war. The Scriptures later identify this global conflict as the fearsome Armageddon.

But after this seemingly final devastation (Joel goes on), there would be a marvelous time of blessing for Israel. God would dwell with his people and they would prosper:

And it shall come to pass afterward, that I will pour out my spirit upon all flesh; and your sons and your daughters shall prophesy, your old men shall dream dreams, your young men shall see visions:

And also upon the servants and upon the handmaids in those days will I pour out my Spirit. (Joel 2:28–29)

Joel's brevity is belied by the enormity of his visions and the pristine beauty of his writing. His book, a mere three chapters, is a model of clarity and force, and his description of Armageddon, along with the hopeful note sounded thereafter, is one of the unforgettable passages of Old Testament prophecy:

Multitudes, multitudes in the valley of decision: for the day of the Lord is near in the valley of decision.

The sun and the moon shall be darkened, and the stars shall withdraw their shining.

The Lord also shall roar out of Zion, and utter his voice from Jerusalem; and the heavens and the earth shall shake: but the

Lord will be the hope of his people, and the strength of the children of Israel. (Joel 3:14–16)

THE RELUCTANT MISSIONARY

The odd ministry of the prophet Jonah provides a rationale for many doubters of the Old Testament record. Truly, the Book of Jonah provides a whale of a story.

Some eighty years before the Assyrian army invaded Israel, the Lord called Jonah to journey to Nineveh, the Assyrian capital, and warn them of God's judgment. But, instead of dutifully heading northeast toward Nineveh, which was situated on the Tigris River in what is now Iraq, Jonah sneaked west to the seaport of Joppa to board a ship bound for Tarshish (Spain?), across the Mediterranean Sea.

He was otherwise a faithful worshipper of God. Though he was a Galilean from the northern kingdom, it is probable that he served the Lord in the Jerusalem Temple, since the record says he fled "from the presence of the Lord," and later promised to return to the "Holy Temple" (Jon. 1:3). Here was a case of a member of the northern tribes who could not stomach the paganism of the north.

But his faith did not extend to accommodating the Gentiles. As a Hebrew he had an aversion to all Gentiles, and particularly to the detested Assyrians. Had not the respected prophet Joel already certified the Assyrians as the dread enemies of Israel? Jonah was loath to obey the Lord in a ministry to Nineveh.

There is a slight hint of a different reason for Jonah's avoidance of the Lord's command (Jon. 4:2). Jonah might have assumed that if he actually did minister to the Assyrians, God might forgive and spare that cruel and dreadful nation. Given a choice, this very human prophet would rather have seen Assyria fall than to personally provide the Lord's mercy for them.

At any rate, Jonah shipped out with pagan Phoenicians, whose company he apparently preferred to the Assyrians. When the craft was well at sea, a ferocious storm hit and the merchant seamen feared for their lives. Experienced at the hazards of navigating the

Mediterranean, the Phoenicians were still overwhelmed by the storm and they began to suspect that its strength indicated the displeasure of the gods. They went about the ship, seeking the cause, as Jonah tried to sleep away his guilt.

It was a dramatic scene with the sailors each calling upon their favorite gods, the ship tossing wildly in the angry sea, and the captain searching frantically for any solution to this spiritual dilemma. Eventually, the skipper came upon the sleeping Hebrew:

So the shipmaster came to him, and said unto him, What meanest thou, O sleeper? arise, call upon thy God, if so be that God will think upon us, that we perish not.

And they said every one to his fellow, Come, and let us cast lots, that we may know for whose cause this evil is upon us. So they cast lots, and the lot fell upon Jonah.

Then said they unto him, Tell us, we pray thee, for whose cause this evil is upon us; What is thine occupation? and whence comest thou? what is thy country? and of what people art thou? (Jon. 1:6–8)

Jonah owned up to the whole story:

And he said unto them, I am an Hebrew; and I fear the Lord, the God of heaven, which hath made the sea and the dry land. (Jon. 1:9)

And he confessed that he had fled from the presence of his God.

Then said they unto him, What shall we do unto thee, that the sea may be calm unto us? for the sea wrought, and was tempestuous. (Jon. 1:11)

The wretched Jonah offered his own life for the sake of the innocent seamen who were suffering because of his sin:

And he said unto them, Take me up, and cast me forth into the sea; so shall the sea be calm unto you: for I know that for my sake this great tempest is upon you. (Jon. 1:12)

At first, the Phoenicians tried hard to row their boat against the winds and high seas and bring it to port, but the job was hopeless. And then, finally, in a rather incredible turnabout, the pagan Phoenicians directly addressed the God of Israel, and, in their desperation, accepted Jonah's plan:

Nevertheless the men rowed hard to bring it to the land; but they could not: for the sea wrought, and was tempestuous against them.

Wherefore they cried unto the Lord, and said, We beseech thee, O Lord, we beseech thee, let us not perish for this man's life, and lay not upon us innocent blood: for thou, O Lord, hast done as it pleased thee.

So they took up Jonah, and cast him forth into the sea: and the sea ceased from her raging. (Jon. 1:13–15)

Apparently, Jonah, who found it so obnoxious to testify to Gentiles in Assyria, had brought the Phoenicians to a healthy fear of the true God:

Then the men feared the Lord exceedingly, and offered a sacrifice unto the Lord, and made vows. (Jon. 1:16)

There follows that singular verse of Scripture that has inspired Sunday School children, turned off unbelievers, and provided so juicy a morsel for the self-styled "higher critics" of the Bible:

Now the Lord had prepared a great fish to swallow up Jonah. And Jonah was in the belly of the fish three days and three nights. (Jon. 1:17)

It is interesting that the Old Testament record does not speak of a whale, but of a great fish. From inside the belly of the fish, Jonah thanks the Lord for sending the creature to save him from drowning at the bottom of the turbulent sea:

The waters compassed me about, even to the soul: the depth closed me round about, the weeds were wrapped about my head.

I went down to the bottoms of the mountains; the earth with her bars was about me for ever: yet hast thou brought up my life from corruption, O Lord my God. (Jon. 2:5–6)

After praying a grand entreaty of repentance, Jonah was expelled from his unique lifeboat.

We can well believe that Jonah set out on a course due northeast to Nineveh at that point. There was certainly no further disobedience to the Lord, and we gather that the Phoenician ship survived the storm.

At Nineveh, Jonah preached that the huge walled metropolis would be destroyed in forty days if the people did not repent before God. And, somehow, they believed him. It is a singular miracle of the Old Testament that an entire city of Gentiles took seriously the admonitions of a Hebrew prophet, but, from the King on down, the Ninevites trusted in Jonah. They called a general fast of repentance before the Almighty: "and put on sackcloth, from the greatest of them even to the least of them" (Jon. 3:5).

The King himself was not above repentance:

For word came unto the king of Nineveh, and he arose from his throne, and he laid his robe from him, and covered him with sackcloth, and sat in ashes. (Jon. 3:6)

The faith of Nineveh circumvented its destruction:

And God saw their works, that they turned from their evil way; and God repented of the evil, that he had said that he would do unto them; and he did it not. (Jon. 3:10)

But now Jonah becomes noticeably resentful of the Lord's mercy. "Why should Nineveh be spared?" he protests. The small Book of Jonah ends on a peculiar note, with God Almighty reasoning with his crestfallen prophet:

And should not I spare Nineveh, that great city, wherein are more than sixscore thousand persons that cannot discern between their right hand and their left hand; and also much cattle? (Jon. 4:11)

THE PRINCE OF THE PROPHETS

The mighty Isaiah now enters the Biblical record. He is a towering figure among Old Testament personalities. His magnificent book, more lengthy than any other prophetic book, gives clear and eloquent pictures of his own age, Israel in exile, the eventual return from Babylon, the manifestation of the Messiah, the blessing of the Gentiles, the return and rule of the Messiah in the Kingdom Age, and, finally, a description of eternity—that mysterious period which consummates all of God's plans.

The Book of Isaiah bears a curious physical resemblance to the Bible as a whole. The entire Bible is comprised of sixty-six books; thirty-nine in the Old Testament, and twenty-seven in the New Testament. The Book of Isaiah is comprised of sixty-six chapters; thirty-nine record the suffering of Israel, including the Babylonian exile, and the following twenty-seven, beginning with the heartening Scripture "Comfort ye, comfort ye my people, saith your God" (Isa. 40:1), record the final triumph of God's plan. The Book of Isaiah has been regarded as a miniature of the entire Biblical record.

Isaiah enjoyed a long and fruitful ministry of sixty years in Judah in the eighth century B.C. He saw the Assyrian destruction of Israel, and he served under four different Kings in Jerusalem. Unlike the wandering pauper prophets that preceded him, Isaiah was of the upper class. He was a priest of the Lord, and had free access to the courts and palaces of the Kings. His extremely comprehensive pictures and forecasts landed with as much effect upon the rulers and subjects of his time as they do on us today.

Isaiah begins his writing with Jehovah's case against Judah. Through Isaiah, God cries out:

Hear, O heavens, and give ear, O earth: for the Lord hath spoken, I have nourished and brought up children, and they have rebelled against me. (Isa. 1:2)

It seemed that the people were still doing their sacrifices and required worship, but that their entire approach to God had become merely ritualistic:

To what purpose is the multitude of your sacrifices unto me? saith the Lord: I am full of the burnt offerings of rams, and the fat of fed beasts; and I delight not in the blood of bullocks, or of lambs, or of he goats. (Isa. 1:11)

Injustice was rampant in the land and widows and orphans were being oppressed, while the oblations in the Temple had become meaningless. The people had utterly overlooked the spirit of the law. Worst of all, idol worship had crept into Judah in the manner that it had completely overtaken Israel (Isa. 1:29).

Through Isaiah, God warns Judah that it, too, will be destroyed for its rebellion against the Lord. One ray of hope is sounded that the Messiah, Immanuel, will be born of a virgin, and will become the Counselor and Mighty God of Israel on earth (Isa. 7:14; 9:6–7).

Then Isaiah turns to the Gentiles, warning them that their fate is no better than that of Judah. They will be judged for their sins, too—whether Babylonia, Philistia, Assyria, Moab, Syria, Ethiopia, Egypt, Arabia, or Tyre—all will have their judgment. In his copious pronouncements, Isaiah seemed to omit no one. The standard he usually applied to Gentile behavior was the way they treated Israel, the chosen of God (Isa. 13:19; 14:1–2).

So much for Judah and the Gentiles. Isaiah now turns his attention to Israel, the northern kingdom, which he calls Ephraim (the name of the largest tribe of the north). He mourns its coming destruction by Assyria. Isaiah lived to see this prophecy fulfilled in 721 B.C., when the ten tribes were led into captivity (Isa. 28:1–3).

There is comfort in Isaiah's message, however. God still loves His people, Isaiah relates, in spite of all of the deterioration, and there will be redemption ahead for Judah and Israel. The nation will suffer, but the Messiah, the Servant of the Lord, will also suffer on their behalf. Through His sacrifice will come the salvation of the Hebrew people.

The prophet urges everyone to comfort the beleaguered Chosen People because they, indeed, will suffer through the judgments of Jehovah. But when all punishments are done with and all accounts paid in full, God will issue forth great blessings. Through the Messiah's suffering atonement, the nation will be exulted and will enter into a glorious kingdom age of righteousness, joy, peace, and prosperity. Isaiah's pictures of the triumphant kingdom age are perhaps nowhere paralleled in Scripture for sheer beauty, promise, and joy.

In the midst of his prophetic discourses, Isaiah digresses to describe the historical situation concerning his beloved friend, King Hezekiah, who had done so much to restore faith in the Lord to Judah. It was Isaiah who had come forward with the prediction of the plague upon the Assyrian army when they confidently besieged Jerusalem. While the King of Judah himself suffered in anguish about the possibility of the destruction of Jerusalem, Isaiah alone remained calm and comforted in the full knowledge that the Almighty would deal with Assyria (Isa. 37:6–7).

It is a hopeless task to explain the magnificent poetry, the lofty visions, and the unerring accuracy of the writings of Isaiah. His estimations of God, his pictures of the Messiah, his majestic promises of the redemption of the Chosen Nation, his constant lessons of the folly of idolatry, and his overwhelming scenes of the glorious future to come to all mankind defy adequate description. The Book of Isaiah must be read to be appreciated.

The United Nations Building in New York City is inscribed with a portion of one of Isaiah's grandest pronouncements:

And he shall judge among the nations, and shall rebuke many people: and they shall beat their swords into plowshares, and their spears into pruninghooks: nation shall not lift up sword against nation, neither shall they learn war any more. (Isa. 2:4)

THE PROPHET OF DOOM

Jeremiah lived a long life of misery and frustration. It was his melancholy task to tell Jerusalem and Judah about the coming destruction of the Temple and the captivity in Babylon.

Jeremiah, the softhearted, weeping prophet from Anathoth, some five miles from Jerusalem, walked the streets of the Holy City in deepest lamentation before an uncaring and unfeeling populace.

He had begun his ministry during the reign of Josiah, so that indeed there was respect for Jehovah abroad in the land. But it seemed that Judah would just not believe that its destruction was nigh. That the ten tribes of the north had fallen was understandable in their view, because of the miserable idolatry of Israel. But Judah, they felt in their spiritual pride, would see no such fate. The weary Jeremiah constantly spoke to deaf ears:

To whom shall I speak, and give warning, that they may hear? behold, their ear is uncircumcised, and they cannot hearken: behold, the word of the Lord is unto them a reproach; they have no delight in it.

Therefore I am full of the fury of the Lord; I am weary with holding in: I will pour it out upon the children abroad, and upon the assembly of young men together: for even the husband with the wife shall be taken, the aged with him that is full of days.

And their houses shall be turned unto others, with their fields and wives together: for I will stretch out my hand upon the inhabitants of the land, saith the Lord. (Jer. 6:10–12)

It should be appreciated that Jeremiah's forewarnings came very briefly before the actual events, so that in this case people who had heard the prophet could validate his accuracy. It was actually only twenty years before the Babylonian siege that the prophet sounded his largely ignored warnings. Like Isaiah, he was a prophet of coming destruction, but, again like Isaiah, he was a prophet to the Gentiles as well as to the Hebrews. Jeremiah too announced that the attitude of Israel's neighbors toward the Chosen People would lead to their own destruction. He clearly warned Egypt, Philistia, Moab, Edom, Arabia, Elam, and Babylonia (Jer. 51:49).

The prophet grew very unpopular as his ministry progressed. No one wanted to hear the daily bad news from Jeremiah, and as much as he loved Jerusalem and his people, he became the most despised man in the city. Eventually, he was accused of being a traitor because of his constant pronouncements against Jerusalem and the Temple. A peculiar trial was held with the priests of the land seeking the blood of Jeremiah, and the stricken prophet only begging them to heed the Word of the Lord. His accusers stopped short of execution and Jeremiah was thrown into prison (Jer. 19:14–20:2; 37:11–21; 38:1–6).

The unwelcomed voice of Jeremiah had been stilled in the streets now, but the prophet went on in his dungeon, composing additional prophecies.

Babylon and Nebuchadnezzar arrived on schedule. Jerusalem was conquered and the Temple thrown down. Zedekiah was installed on the throne of the ruined kingdom, as a puppet king controlled from Babylon. The puppet king released Jeremiah from the dungeon and placed him under more comfortable house arrest. But since he continued to preach complete surrender to the Babylonians—in accordance with the Will of God—the people threw him into a pit. Jeremiah knew nothing but total unacceptance throughout his long career.

When Jerusalem was totally destroyed in 586 B.C., King Nebuchadnezzar gave Jeremiah the option of going to Babylon with the captive upper class, or remaining in Judah with the poor remnant left behind. The prophet elected to remain in the ruins of the Holy City and to try to continue to minister to those few Nebuchadnezzar saw fit to leave in the land.

Every year, on the ninth day of the month of Av, the people of Israel and Jewish people the world over weep through Jeremiah's Book of Lamentations in a special day of mourning. The Temple was indeed destroyed as Jeremiah predicted, on that day in 586 B.C., and the Second Temple, in which the Messiah taught, was also destroyed on the ninth of Av (A.D. 70). The veracity of Jeremiah has been vindicated through the centuries by the descendants of those who would not hear him in his time.

Now, the destruction of the Hebrew people seemed complete. All of the talented tradesmen, military leaders, and educated populace of Judah were captive and were taken to Babylon, and only the poorest sort of landworkers remained in Jerusalem. This was the way Nebuchadnezzar had insured a comfortable reign over his new province.

The remnant finally left Jerusalem for Egypt, seeing no point to remaining in the wreckage of what had once been one of the most glorious capital cities of the known world. Jeremiah went along with them and probably died there, outside of the land he made every effort to save.

One bright note in Jeremiah's prophecy was his teaching of the return of Judah. He prophesied that the Jewish people would be released from the land of Babylon after seventy years' captivity, and that ultimately there would be a New Covenant between God and Israel that would be eternal (Jer. 25:11–12; 29:10; 31:31–34).

Jeremiah's accuracy, scope, and poetry virtually equal the timeless pronouncements of Isaiah. He was one of the brilliant men of the prophetic period, however unappreciated he was. His ultimate messages, which, like Isaiah's, reached well beyond his own time and into the kingdom age, leave us with a hopeful feeling after all is said and done. His Book of Lamentations, on the other hand, sounds a note of despair unequaled in the Scriptures. The testing of Job and the profound frustration of Ecclesiastes are perhaps the only other Scriptural poems that reach the sorrow and the pity sung by the faithful Jeremiah.

OTHER VOICES OF THE LORD

There were many other prophets who lived and taught and wrote the message of God in Judah and Israel during the four centuries of the Hebrew Kings, of course. We have tried to cover the high points and the important works of the greater prophets. (Later prophets of the exile and return to the land will be covered in the next chapter.)

The lesser, or so-called minor, prophets wrote smaller books, but not less emphatic messages. Hosea taught that God loves Israel as a man loves his wife, even if she is unfaithful to him. Micah, a contemporary of Isaiah, described Assyria as the instrument of God's wrath, but promised that there would be a glorious future under the Messiah during His righteous reign. Nahum predicted the awesome destruction of fallen Nineveh, about a century after Jonah's ministry there. The contentious Jonah would have felt vindicated, at last.

Zephaniah, a descendant of the great King Hezekiah and a contemporary of Jeremiah, taught that the impending destruction of Jerusalem was but a foreshadowing of the future "Day of the Lord," or Tribulation, but that there would ultimately be joy when the Messiah, the King of Israel, would reign (Zeph. 3:15). Habakkuk, also a contemporary of Jeremiah, argued with God about His use of the vicious and idolatrous Babylonians to discipline Jerusalem. God responded that Judah had to be punished for its sins, but that "the just shall live by faith" (Hab. 2:4). This deathless saying of the minor prophet Habakkuk is certainly one of the structural pillars of the New Testament.

Obadiah, who wrote his brief contribution shortly after the destruction of Jerusalem, warned neighboring Edom that a similar fate awaited them for their pride and their violence against Israel.

Thus, the prophets of the Lord came forth and did their unique works during times of various idolatries and fitful periods of genuine faith. Occasionally their messages were heeded, with profit to the people, but, by and large, the populace of both kingdoms preferred to hear the call of Gentile gods and pagan priests. There was so much bowing down to false deities that the Lord was forced to punish both parts of the divided nation.

The theme of the books of the prophets is that the Chosen People had forgotten their exalted calling, as the keepers of the law of God, and instead became influenced, as was King Solomon, the beginning of it all, by the base traditions of the surrounding nations. They would emerge again to spiritual greatness only under the coming Messiah.

God's punishment fit the crime. Both Israel and Judah ended in captivity in Assyria and Babylon, respectively, the heartland of idolatry and paganism in the known world.

10

Israel in Agony:
Exile and Rebirth

That God would ever destroy His own Holy City and His own Temple was simply incomprehensible to the people of Judah. Forewarned as they were by the prophets, and obviously quite conscious of their shortcomings before the Lord, they were still totally surprised by the assault of Babylon.

For some eight hundred years, the Hebrew people had successfully occupied the Promised Land (longer than the rise and fall of Greece and Rome together). From the time of Joshua and the original pilgrims from the wilderness, to the days of Jeremiah, the Hebrew culture, language, and populace had been the dominant feature of that one-of-a-kind territory. The Judges, Kings, prophets, and priests had left an indelible mark on history, and the renowned Jerusalem Temple was respected throughout the ancient world.

True, they had wars with the surrounding peoples and had their own internal struggles with government, the paganism that threatened them on every side, and all of the normal ups and downs of the human condition. They had paid tribute to various powerful foreign governments, they had seen the ten northern tribes decimated and deported to Assyria, but, somehow, Judah now felt secure as the Chosen People in the Promised Land.

But at the beginning of the sixth century B.C., it was all to vanish. The beauty, grace, worship, law, and culture of the Hebrew people was to disappear from the land of Israel, and total desolation was to replace it. Though God still loved His special children and His Holy City, He could no longer tolerate the rebellion, injustice, and evil in the land. With abundant forewarnings from the prophets, He allowed the terrible Nebuchadnezzar to breach the protective shield the Lord had placed around Judah and to destroy Jerusalem and the Temple. The populace of Judah, the remnant of the original exodus from Egypt, was carried away into captivity in Babylon.

THE FALL OF JERUSALEM

The invasion by Nebuchadnezzar actually came in three stages. Perhaps the King of Babylon did not really want to destroy Jerusalem, a showplace of the Middle East. He would rather have just taken tribute from it than make it rubble. But when he tried to assert his might against the city, the reigning King, Jehoiakim, rebelled and the Babylonians entered Jerusalem. In 606 B.C., Nebuchadnezzar took Jehoiakim captive to Babylon, along with high officers of his court. This is referred to in the record as the first deportation (II Chron. 36:5–7; Dan. 1:1–4). Nebuchadnezzar installed the youthful Jehoiachin, the son of Jehoiakim, as King.

In 597 B.C., Nebuchadnezzar came back in his second reign of terror and besieged Jerusalem. On this occasion, he took the eighteen-year-old King Jehoiachin into captivity. The King, along with all of the military leaders, princes, and skilled craftsmen of Judah, was taken away. Fully ten thousand people were marched a thousand miles back to Nebuchadnezzar's capital! Babylon intended to leave only the poorest people in Jerusalem and Judah in order to maintain complete control over the territory (II Kings 24:10–16). Zedekiah, Jehoiachin's uncle, became King over what was left of Judah, and ruled by orders from Babylon.

In 586 B.C., Zedekiah rebelled against Nebuchadnezzar. The Babylonian King was beginning to appreciate that the Hebrew people were hard to oppress, and this time, he brought a huge army to Jerusalem and suffocated the city in a seven-month siege. There was starvation in the streets in Jerusalem while Nebuchadnezzar's army surrounded the walls. King Zedekiah tried to slip away by night and break for Jericho, but was apprehended by a detachment of the Chaldees. His fate was to see his sons killed before his eyes, and then be blinded and carried off to Babylon in brass fetters.

It must have only been a relief when the Babylonians finally entered Jerusalem and utterly leveled the city. They destroyed the Temple, tore down the huge walls, and left merely hillsides and fields of broken stone (II Kings 25:8–10).

The Promised Land was no more, at least as far as the Chosen People were concerned. The omnipresent tribes of pagans now occupied Israel. And ordinary historical logic would tell us that the Hebrews would never likely return.

PROPHET TO THE KING

But God had not forgotten His Chosen People, even in their exile. Prophets rose up, just as in former times, and ministered to the captives. An adolescent prince of Jerusalem's royal court called Daniel was among those taken prisoner during the first deportation, along with King Jehoiakim. Noticeably intelligent and sensitive, Daniel was given favored status, along with a few others from Jerusalem, and placed in the University of Babylon to be educated. A privileged few of various conquered nations were to serve as advisors to King Nebuchadnezzar. In contrast to the brutality of the Babylonian armies in the field, the court was rather humane in such customs.

Daniel, like his ancestor Joseph of the Land of Egypt over a thousand years before, was gifted by the Lord in the ministry of interpreting dreams. He was also faithful to the God of Israel and His law, even in the strange surroundings of the Babylonian court:

But Daniel purposed in his heart that he would not defile himself with the portion of the king's meat, nor with the wine which he drank: therefore he requested of the prince of the eunuchs that he might not defile himself. (Dan. 1:8)

One night, King Nebuchadnezzar experienced a disturbing dream. He called all of his advisors, magicians, and mediums together and informed them that he had forgotten his dream, but was deeply troubled about it. He demanded that they tell him the dream and then interpret it.

The King's advisors replied tactfully to the difficult order:

> Then spake the Chaldeans to the king in Syriack, O king, live for ever: tell thy servants the dream, and we will shew the interpretation. (Dan. 2:4)

It was only a reasonable request; how in the world could they know the King's dream at all, let alone interpret it? But Nebuchadnezzar was used to having his way. He presents them with quite an incentive to work diligently on the assignment:

> The king answered and said to the Chaldeans, The thing is gone from me: if ye will not make known unto me the dream, with the interpretation thereof, ye shall be cut in pieces, and your houses shall be made a dunghill. (Dan. 2:5)

The discussion goes back and forth for quite some time, until the panicky wisemen own up to their lack of skill:

> The Chaldeans answered before the king, and said, There is not a man upon the earth that can shew the king's matter: therefore there is no king, lord, nor ruler, that asked such things at any magician, or astrologer, or Chaldean. (Dan. 2:10)

The petulant Nebuchadnezzar had an answer for that one, too. He issued a decree that all wisemen in Babylon be executed (Dan. 2:12–13).

When Daniel heard this decree, he understood very well that the execution would include himself, as a dream-interpreter-in-training, as well as his Hebrew compatriots. He went to the Lord with the matter. Confidently, he also sent a message to the King to hold off the execution since he, Daniel, would shortly tell the King his dream and its interpretation. God answered Daniel's prayer, meanwhile, revealing the remarkable dream He had given to Nebuchadnezzar, along with its meaning.

Nebuchadnezzar, like Joseph's Pharaoh back in Egypt, was intrigued and agreed to an audience with the youthful Hebrew.

In a scene not unlike that in Pharaoh's throneroom when Joseph stood before the monarch of Egypt, the King cautiously inquired of Daniel, "Art thou able to make known unto me the dream which I have seen, and the interpretation thereof?" Daniel answered in the presence of the King, and said, "The secret which the King hath demanded cannot the wise men, the astrologers, the magicians, the soothsayers, shew unto the King; But there is a God in heaven that revealeth secrets, and maketh known to the King Nebuchadnezzar what shall be in the latter days" (Dan. 2:26-28).

In almost the very words of his illustrious ancestor, Daniel taught the pagan King that the answer was to be found in the God of Israel.

Daniel was as good as his claims, and he told the King his dream and then interpreted it. (Conceivably, Nebuchadnezzar had not forgotten his dream at all, but wanted to test the accuracy of his seers. In any case, he was deeply impressed with the performance of Daniel.)

The dream, well worth close study, might be called "History in a Statue." Nebuchadnezzar had dreamed of a gigantic metallic statue of a man, and a flying stone which struck the statue on the feet. The statue crumbled into dust and was blown away when it was hit by the stone. Daniel said that Nebuchadnezzar had dreamed nothing less than the entire political future of the world, from that day until the end of time. His breath-taking interpretation showed that all history—or the future, from his point of view—was divided into the rule of five successive great kingdoms. This was shown in the statue, which had a head of gold, torso and arms of silver, thighs of bronze, legs of iron, and feet of mixed iron and clay. The four metals depicted four successive human kingdoms, or world powers, and the stone represented the future Kingdom of God that would ultimately destroy human rule and occupy the earth. The four human powers, Daniel analyzed, were, in order of appearance (as Daniel gave them), Babylonia (the head), Medo-Persia (torso and arms), Greece (thighs), and Rome (legs continuing on down through the feet in its current mixed condition until the Kingdom of God is established on the earth) (Dan. 2:31-45).

If Nebuchadnezzar was impressed at the accuracy of Daniel (which he was), it's too bad he cannot look at the dream from our perspective today. The empires indeed rose and fell exactly as Daniel predicted, with the Kingdom of God coming some time in our own future.

The King rewarded Daniel and gave him a very high position as a result of his wisdom and divine insight.

But Daniel's new associates in the royal court quickly grew tired of the devout Jew among them, who never forsook his faithfulness to the God of Israel. After King Darius of Persia had taken power over Babylon (representing Medo-Persia, the torso and arms of Nebuchadnezzar's dream statue), they encouraged Darius to pass a decree that no one be permitted to pray to any other god than the King himself. Daniel felt obliged to ignore this law, and kept up his normal prayer schedule with his face turned westward toward Jerusalem three times each day. After being apprehended at his prayers, Daniel was thrown into a den of lions, to be torn and eaten. The plot fell through, of course, when the Lord pacified the ravenous beasts, and Daniel emerged very much alive and in prayer the next morning (Dan. 6:7–11, 22).

Daniel lived a long and faithful life in Babylon, always praying for the freedom of the Jewish people and the return to the Promised Land. He studied the Book of Jeremiah carefully, and learned that Israel's captivity would last seventy years (Dan. 9:2; Jer. 29:10).

But the Lord sent an angel in response to Daniel's supplication who revealed that the Lord was now establishing a much more comprehensive timetable. The present seventy-year captivity would be ended on schedule, but, more importantly, the Lord was now going to undertake a very lengthy schedule of "seventy weeks of years," or seventy sets of seven years each (490 years). By the end of that period, all things concerning Israel and Jerusalem would be completely fulfilled (Dan. 9:24). The 490-year period was subdivided into certain climactic events, which would guarantee the accuracy of the prophecy as time went on. By the end of forty-nine years, Jerusalem was to be rebuilt. At the end of 483 years, the Messiah would come and be killed. After that, the Temple, which would have been rebuilt in the meanwhile, would be destroyed. The final seven years would begin with a covenant between a future Evil Prince and Israel, and conclude with the final devastating war, Armageddon (Dan. 9:24–27).

There is not space here to analyze fully the magnificent "seventy weeks of years" prophecy, which sweeps through the centuries with those identifiable stops along the way. The time of the first coming of Christ, the Jewish Messiah, can be calculated with this prophecy, as well as the rebuilding of Jerusalem and the destruction of the Second Temple. Jewish history has worked out in exact conformity to this marvelous prophecy and world history will undoubtedly conform to its final passages.*

Daniel's book is filled with cryptic visions, interspersed with interpretations by the Lord Himself, which certainly help the reader. The book uniquely correlates with Revelation, the final book of the New Testament, in its pictures of the coming end times. Images, numbers, time periods, and political situations as seen by Daniel are corroborated in Revelation, and the two books, written centuries apart in different lands by quite different people, appear to have been taken from the same source.

And, of course, they were, since all Biblical prophecy is ultimately authored by God.

Daniel lived to see Cyrus, King of Persia, decree that the people of Israel could return to the land and rebuild their Temple of God. The seventy-year period was over, and hearty pioneers among the Hebrews journeyed back to the ruins of their Holy City to begin the hard work. As for the now aged Daniel, he lived out his last few years in the royal court, and died in peace in Babylon.

PROPHET TO THE PEOPLE

Ezekiel was another one of God's key men carried off to Babylon. While Daniel was a prophet to Kings, Ezekiel ministered among his own captive people in the strange land.

If Daniel, the former Judaean prince and now prophet to the royal court of Babylon, held a position like that of Joseph in

---

* See *Satan in the Sanctuary*, by the authors, Moody Press, 1973, for the complete calculations.

Egypt, then Ezekiel was more like Moses. He worked among the common folk and was simply one of the exiled ones.

The Hebrew people lived and labored along the banks of the Chebar River, which was actually a man-made commercial canal between the Tigris and Euphrates. Undoubtedly, the captive Hebrews were engaged in the forced labor connected with the heavy traffic on the great Mesopotamian canal.

It seemed now that paganism became obnoxious to the Jewish people. Jerusalem and the Temple of God were an agonizing memory in the minds of those who had been dragged in chains to Babylon, and the new generation, born in exile, saw all around them the total corruption of idol worship. They abhorred the ways of the Babylonians as emphatically as their ancestors of Judah had admired the Gentile nations and went after their idols. The godly among the captives tried to worship the Lord and keep the law as best they could, away from the Temple. The captivity, all in all, had a purgative effect on the Chosen People. Like children being disciplined, they were learning their lesson well. Ezekiel the priest was in their midst, "sitting where they sat," and God revealed through him that the exiled Jewish people were still His people. Ezekiel reiterated to his generation just why God had allowed the pagans to overwhelm Judah and Jerusalem and lay waste the House of the Lord.

Ezekiel was called into service through a remarkable vision the Lord gave him. Few prophets enjoyed the spectacular visions of Ezekiel, in general, and his initial calling has fascinated Bible believers, and unbelievers, over the millennia. Ezekiel saw an incredible combination of flashing lights, winds, angelic creatures with wings, concentric wheels, and the very Throne of God; and he also experienced the overwhelming voice of the Almighty (Ezek. 1:4–25). Some imaginative Bible readers have tried to construe spaceships, UFO's, and other exotic phenomena as being the real meaning of Ezekiel's experience, but nothing in the record supports this. It must be borne in mind that these things were seen by Ezekiel in a vision; they were not real-life events.

In any case, out of this heavenly extravaganza, the stupefied Ezekiel was called into prophetic service. But had he foreseen the terrible difficulties of his coming ministry, he might well have begged off. Ezekiel was a one-man drama of disaster; he was obliged by the Lord actually to act out in front of the people the punishments and tragedies of Israel's disobedience.

Ezekiel was unpopular, to say the least, when he described the judgment of God against Jerusalem. As a matter of fact, the people refused to listen. As a result, Ezekiel was struck dumb; since he could no longer speak, he was to dramatize the messages of God in the manner of a mime.

To depict the siege and destruction of the Holy City, the mute prophet drew a map of Jerusalem on a clay tile, built up clay mounds around it to represent the siege, and put a frying pan turned sideways between him and his model city. He then lay down on his left side for 390 days, to show the number of years of the judgment on Jerusalem and God's refusal to rise in its defense. Ezekiel's silent shows, demanding as they were on the prophet himself, made more impact on the people than his vocal presentations (Ezek. 4:1–8).

The prophet's wife died, but God refused to allow him to mourn. Ezekiel was forced to eat bread baked over human dung. All of these arduous demonstrations caused the people at least to notice Ezekiel's message, although he was considered by some to be simply insane.

In another vision, Ezekiel was taken back to Solomon's Temple and shown the "abominations" of idolatry that had been conducted in the very House of the Lord and had, of course, brought down the wrath of God on the city and the nation (Ezek. 8:5–18). One of the most sorrowful and moving scenes in the entire Old Testament occurred to Ezekiel in a further vision. It showed the actual departure of the Shekinah Glory of God—that dependable cloud that had attended the Tabernacle and the Temple—from the House of the Lord. The glorious cloud rose up from the Ark of the Covenant in the Holy of Holies, the most sacred room of the Temple, lingered at the East Gate of the Temple wall, hovered over the Mount of Olives overlooking the city, and then finally ascended to heaven (Ezek. 10:18, 19; 11:22–23). How reluctant the Almighty was to withdraw from His people; how strikingly similar to the ascension of Christ from the "City of the Great King" six hundred years later.

In the style of the other major prophets before him, Ezekiel, after excoriating the Jewish nation for their rebellion and sin, then turned his prophetic attention to the surrounding Gentile nations. Ezekiel showed that the same God who judged Israel will also judge them—to a large extent by the way they have treated God's Chosen People.

Through Ezekiel, God prophesied against the Ammonites, Moab, Edom, Philistia, and particularly the great coastal Phoenician city of Tyre. The people of Tyre were delighted when Jerusalem was destroyed, feeling that they would prosper with the demise of the competitive Jewish capital (Ezek. 26:2–3). God was not pleased with this attitude, to say the least. Ezekiel, his verbal powers restored, announced that nations would attack Tyre, "destroy the walls and break down her towers." They would scrape her dust, flatten the city, and "make her like the top of a rock. It shall be a place for spreading of nets" (Ezek. 26:3–5).

As things worked out, Nebuchadnezzar, the vanquisher of Jerusalem, turned on Tyre and fulfilled the first part of the prophecy; he tore down the walls and towers of the great seafaring city and dispersed the population. Many of the people, however, escaped safely to an island offshore. But three hundred years later, the fierce Alexander the Great fulfilled the second part of the prophecy. When the mighty conqueror confronted Tyre, he saw a peculiar situation—an ancient mainland city, largely in ruins, and the populace camped on the island away from the coast. There were treacherous shoals in the water, and Alexander elected not to use ships. Instead, he had his army utilize the stones and soil of mainland Tyre to build a causeway out to the island. Alexander's men were thorough; so thorough, in fact, that they completely cleaned out all stones from ancient Tyre, so that the city was left flat and clean, "like the top of a rock." The laborious assault was finally successful, and fishermen still today spread their nets out for drying and repair on the convenient flat rock that was once the metropolis of Tyre.

The passage certainly demonstrates the precision of prophecy. Fishermen would never have considered putting in to busy ancient Tyre for the spreading and repair of large fishing nets, of course, but when God fulfilled His curse, the site was ideal for that purpose, and still is. Tyre should never have rejoiced over the destruction of God's Holy City.

Typical of the foregoing prophets, Ezekiel then turns his attention to the distant future, the last days, in which he envisions the restoration of Israel from a vast worldwide dispersion of the Jews. Obviously, we are living in exactly those times. Ezekiel pictures the Jewish people being regathered from the world as if they were dry bones exhumed from the graves of the Gentile nations where they had been scattered (Ezek. 37:11–14). He then foresees an invasion of Israel by a great power from the north (Ezek. 38–39).*

Ultimately, after much further tribulation and war, the Lord will cleanse Israel, Ezekiel foresees, and put His Spirit upon the Jewish people in glory and blessing (Ezek. 37:14).

Ezekiel's final prophecies, from his fortieth chapter on, reveal the magnificence of the Temple of God in the Kingdom Age, when Israel is finally restored and the Davidic Messiah-Shepherd will reign (see Ezek. 34:23–28). This Messianic Temple will be far more splendorous and beautiful than either Solomon's or the Second Temple built by Zerubbabel after the return from Babylon (and remodeled grandly by Herod at the time of Christ).

Ezekiel's prophecies conclude with the final words, "The Lord is there," in his last verse. Nothing is mentioned in the Scriptures about his later life or death.

THE RETURN: ISRAEL REBORN

The seventy years of the Babylonian captivity passed as prophesied. The people of Israel returned, in part, to their Promised Land. There were those, of course, who, raised in Babylon and accustomed to their surroundings, did not choose to return to the pioneer task of rebuilding Israel. Today, as in that time, the greater percentage of the Jews remain in the dispersion rather than returning to rebuild the land.

The Hebrew nation did not simply walk over the borders of Babylon, of course. The reigning King Belshazzar was certainly

* See *The Coming Russian Invasion of Israel*, by the authors, Moody Press, 1974.

not of a mind to restore his former enemies back to their land to rebuild the infernal Temple of their God. It was necessary, in fact, for the Lord to arrange to transfer the Gentile world power from the Babylonians to the Medo-Persians literally *overnight*, as Daniel records (Dan. 5:30–31).

It was a great night for King Belshazzar, that last night of his reign, and of his life. He had thrown "a great feast" for a thousand of his princes and governors gathered from the far-flung realms of the Babylonian Empire. The King's wives and concubines graced the reveling as the party went on far into the night. As the *pièce de résistance* of his entertaining, Belshazzar decided to bring out the sacred vessels of the Jerusalem Temple, which Nebuchadnezzar had confiscated, in order to serve his guests wine:

> Then they brought the golden vessels that were taken out of the temple of the house of God which was at Jerusalem; and the king, and his princes, his wives, and his concubines, drank in them.

> They drank wine, and praised the gods of gold, and of silver, of brass, of iron, of wood, and of stone. (Dan. 5:3–4)

Belshazzar had gone too far, now, as we can well imagine. The God of Israel was not about to permit His sacred artifacts from His own House to be utilized at a pagan orgy. A dramatic scene ensues:

> In the same hour came forth fingers of a man's hand, and wrote over against the candlestick upon the plaister of the wall of the king's palace: and the king saw the part of the hand that wrote.

> Then the king's countenance was changed, and his thoughts troubled him, so that the joints of his loins were loosed, and his knees smote one against another. (Dan. 5:5–6)

To this strange moment, we owe our expression "the handwriting on the wall." Could Belshazzar understand the handwriting on the wall? Not at all. The inscription read: "MENE, MENE, TEKEL, UPHARSIN," and the King and governors were stumped.

Knees knocking, Belshazzar sent for his astrologers, the Chal-

deans, and the soothsayers. The wisemen of Babylon were as sty-
mied before Belshazzar as they had been before Nebuchadnezzar.
No one could interpret the handwriting on the wall. But then, the
Queen came forward with some good advice:

> Now the queen by reason of the words of the king and his lords
> came into the banquet house: and the queen spake and said, O
> king, live for ever: let not thy thoughts trouble thee, nor let thy
> countenance be changed.

> There is a man in thy kingdom, in whom is the spirit of the
> holy gods; and in the days of thy father light and understanding
> and wisdom, like the wisdom of the gods, was found in him;
> whom the king Nebuchadnezzar thy father, the king, I say, thy
> father, made master of the magicians, astrologers, Chaldeans,
> and soothsayers. (Dan. 5:10–11)

The dependable Daniel was brought in, as in the days of yore,
and the King offered him a wonderful reward:

> And I have heard of thee, that thou canst make interpretations,
> and dissolve doubts: now if thou canst read the writing, and
> make known to me the interpretation thereof, thou shalt be
> clothed with scarlet, and have a chain of gold about thy neck,
> and shalt be the third ruler in the kingdom. (Dan. 5:16)

Daniel told the King he didn't care to become a ruler of Babylon, but would oblige with the interpretation. The message is
translated at length in Dan. 5:25–28, but, in substance, it said:

To: Belshazzar
From: God
The party's over!

And, in point of fact, the daring Darius was at that very moment bringing his army through the nearly impregnable double
walls of Babylon. He had dammed up the Euphrates River and
marched from behind the water flow into the city.

Back at the palace, Belshazzar was hanging his silly chain of
gold around the neck of Daniel and making him some sort of
ruler over a pagan territory. The die was cast, however, or, we

should say, "the handwriting was on the wall." Darius was King within a few hours. The patient Daniel never did rule with Belshazzar to his great relief. God, not man, after all, decides who will rule in all nations.

Darius was certified as King of the Babylonians by the Persian overlord, King Cyrus, called the "King of Kings" over the entire empire (Dan. 9:1). Cyrus was a God-fearing King who appeared in the earlier prophecy of Isaiah. He amazed the pagan world by announcing, in his very first year of rule, that the Lord God of Heaven had given him the empire and had ordered him to see that the Temple of God was rebuilt in Jerusalem. He issued a written decree to that effect and commissioned the Jewish people to return and build it. He even encouraged financial assistance for the project.

The benevolent Cyrus issued his decree in writing in the most unmistakable terms:

Thus saith Cyrus king of Persia, The Lord God of heaven hath given me all the kingdoms of the earth; and he hath charged me to build him an house at Jerusalem, which is in Judah.

Who is there among you of all his people? his God be with him, and let him go up to Jerusalem, which is in Judah, and build the house of the Lord God of Israel, (he is the God,) which is in Jerusalem.

And whosoever remaineth in any place where he sojourneth, let the men of his place help him with silver, and with gold, and with goods, and with beasts, beside the freewill offering for the house of God that is in Jerusalem. (Ezra 1:2–4)

Students of Isaiah must have been gratified by this precise fulfillment of prophecy. One hundred and fifty years before King Cyrus came to power, Isaiah had singled out the Persian ruler *by name* as the personality the Lord would use to cause the Temple to be rebuilt:

That saith of Cyrus, He is my shepherd, and shall perform all my pleasure: even saying to Jerusalem, Thou shalt be built; and to the temple, Thy foundation shall be laid. (Isa. 44:28)

For Jacob my servant's sake, and Israel mine elect, I have even called thee by thy name: I have surnamed thee, though thou hast not known me. (Isa. 45:4)

Such exact prophecy has caused skepticism among unbelieving critics, of course. They assume that Isaiah must have been written *after* the time of Cyrus, since it actually named the Persian King. But it is quite possible that some believing Hebrews showed King Cyrus the mention of his name in Isaiah and the God-fearing King hastened to do what the Lord had indicated for him to do. In any case, when the Lord was ready to release His people, He used the instruments that He pleased to use: King of Kings Cyrus, and a massive shift of the power structure of the entire Middle Eastern Empire.

The gold and silver equipment of the Temple, which had been stored in the Babylonian treasury, was released to the Jewish people as they returned to Jerusalem. All twelve tribes were represented. Judah, Benjamin, and Levi were predominant (the original southern kingdom plus the priests). They were led by Zerubbabel, a descendant of King David, who would probably have succeeded to the throne of Judah if the monarchy were re-established. Joshua, the new High Priest, and the prophets Haggai and Zechariah, accompanied the new Jewish immigrants (Ezra 3:8; 5:1).

And so, much chastened, the Israelites returned to their Promised Land, carrying those Temple artifacts which had been the heart and soul of their religion for a thousand years. They determined to make a new start in Israel and they undertook to build the Second Temple of God.

"I WILL FILL THIS HOUSE WITH GLORY"

The work began in earnest and within about five years the foundation of the Temple was laid (c. 536 B.C.). When this was accomplished, there was a ceremony of considerable importance and good cheer:

And when the builders laid the foundation of the temple of the Lord, they set the priests in their apparel with trumpets, and the Levites the sons of Asaph with cymbals, to praise the Lord, after the ordinance of David king of Israel.

And they sang together by course in praising and giving thanks unto the Lord; because he is good, for his mercy endureth forever toward Israel. And all the people shouted with a great shout, when they praised the Lord, because the foundation of the house of the Lord was laid. (Ezra 3:10–11)

The new Temple, however, was to be much smaller than the magnificent House of God built by the wealthy Solomon in much better times. There was a mixed reaction once the foundation was in place and the remnant of Judah could estimate the magnitude of the new Temple:

But many of the priests and Levites and chief of the fathers, who were ancient men, that had seen the first house, when the foundation of this house was laid before their eyes, wept with a loud voice; and many shouted aloud for joy:

So that the people could not discern the noise of the shout of joy from the noise of the weeping of the people: for the people shouted with a loud shout, and the noise was heard afar off. (Ezra 3:12–13)

The prophet Haggai was to greatly cheer on the Temple builders, however. Despite the diminutive size of the Second House of the Lord, God said through Haggai:

And I will shake all nations, and the desire of all nations shall come: and I will fill this house with glory, saith the Lord of hosts.

The silver is mine, and the gold is mine, saith the Lord of hosts.

The glory of this latter house shall be greater than of the former, saith the Lord of hosts: and in this place will I give peace, saith the Lord of hosts. (Hag. 2:7–9)

True enough, as things worked out, for this was the Temple in which the Prince of Peace was to teach.

Of course, laying the foundation and actually building the Temple were different matters. The construction itself took twenty years to accomplish, since the remnant of the Hebrews had constant opposition to the project from their new northern neighbors, the Samaritans (Ezra 4:10). The "Samaritans" were actually a polyglot mixture of odds and ends of people from everywhere in the Assyrian Empire. After the Assyrians had deported the northern ten tribes of Israel, this variety of peoples was moved in to occupy the fertile land. The Assyrians moved whole nations about as one might move herds of grazing animals. There was some intermarriage between the new immigrants and the remaining Israelites, and the resulting generations came to be known as Samaritans. They had their own temple on Mount Gerazim, and were considered apostates from the true worship of God by the authentic Jewish people (see John 4, where Jesus confronts a Samaritan woman).

The Samaritans stood by, stirring up animosity against Judah. They sent an accusatory letter to the then Persian King Artaxerxes, pointing out that Jerusalem had a history of independence and rebellion, and that when the Jews finished rebuilding it they would refuse to pay taxes to the King. Artaxerxes ordered the rebuilding to stop and for several years the Temple construction languished incomplete. Then Haggai and the prophet Zechariah, also on the scene, informed the Hebrews that completing the Temple was the Will of God and they should continue. But again the Samaritans interfered, contacting King Darius, the Persian. Darius, however, searched the archives in Babylon and found the primary decree of King Cyrus ordering the Temple rebuilt. He sided with the Hebrews, and so the Temple was finally finished and dedicated to the Lord in 516 B.C. Thus the time between the destruction of Solomon's Temple in 586, and the completion of the rebuilding in 516, amounted to exactly seventy years, as prophesied by Jeremiah.

Haggai and Zechariah continued to encourage the feeble remnant of Israel in the difficult work of rebuilding the Temple, but they both saw far beyond that current task. Zechariah supplied some of the finest and most extensive prophetic analyses about the great future Kingdom Age of the Messiah. He spoke of the Good Shepherd, who would be rejected, and of God ultimately dropping His protective shield around Jerusalem once more. This prophecy was fulfilled when the Messiah was not received and the Romans destroyed Jerusalem in A.D. 70. Zechariah went on to speak of Armageddon and the second coming of the Messiah, who will cleanse Israel and establish His millennial kingdom on earth (Zech. 12–14).

BEAUTY AND THE BEAST

Most of the Jewish people remained scattered in various parts of the Persian Empire, however. Jerusalem and the Temple were functioning, but not many had returned.

Around 485 B.C., a young Jewess named Esther won a nation-wide beauty contest and became Queen to the Persian King Xerxes (Ahasuerus)—presumably the first prize:

And the king loved Esther above all the women, and she obtained grace and favour in his sight more than all the virgins; so that he set the royal crown upon her head, and made her queen instead of Vashti. (Esther 2:17)

Xerxes considered it absolutely necessary to replace the disobedient Queen Vashti, who had refused to come at his command to show off her great beauty before the people (Esther 1:11–12). The King's counselors advised him that Vashti's poor example might inspire women throughout the empire to disobey their husbands, and they recommended stern measures to the King:

Likewise shall the ladies of Persia and Media say this day unto all the king's princes, which have heard of the deed of the queen. Thus shall there arise too much contempt and wrath.

If it please the king, let there go a royal commandment from him, and let it be written among the laws of the Persians and the Medes, that it be not altered, That Vashti come no more before king Ahasuerus; and let the king give her royal estate unto another that is better than she.

And when the king's decree which he shall make shall be published throughout all his empire, (for it is great,) all the wives shall give to their husbands honour, both to great and small. (Esther 1:18–20)

Thus the Medo-Persian women's liberation movement was nipped in the bud! The King issued the decree, declaring in part, "that every man should bear rule in his own house." He published this royal doctrine in every language of the empire, and at once began the search that turned up the comely Israelite, Esther of Shushan.

Esther kept her lineage a secret and accepted the royal crown. In the meanwhile, the wicked Prime Minister Haman was undertaking a plot of genocide against the Chosen People. In a fascinating story, still rehearsed by the Jews annually on the festival called Purim, Esther disclosed to her husband the plot of the Prime Minister and the fact that she, as a Hebrew, would be killed if Haman's plot were successful. Xerxes was astonished and immediately executed his Prime Minister. The intriguing twists and turns of the little Book of Esther, so very rich and human a story, express in miniature the troubles and the triumphs of God's Chosen People. It is no exaggeration to say that without the courage of Esther and the unique circumstances in the Medo-Persian court, the world would not have the Biblical revelation or the Jewish people (who later included the disciples and the apostles, not to mention the Messiah Himself).

Around 445 B.C., during the reign of the Persian King Artaxerxes Longiminus, the prophets Ezra and Nehemiah went from Babylon and Shushan to Jerusalem to rally the people of Judah. Nehemiah had been a valued personal advisor to Artaxerxes in the Shushan palace, and pleaded with the King for permission to rebuild the walls of the Holy City, which were still in ruins from the destruction by Nebuchadnezzar (Neh. 2). The Temple, of course, was complete, but stood insecurely on an unwalled site. Nehemiah received the royal permission and was able to get the job completed. Jerusalem was again a valid city, walled and secure, and continually attracted more of the Chosen People to settle in their ancient capital.

Ezra held a public reading of the Mosaic law to the people, in the manner of King Josiah before him, and exhorted them to keep it; especially the prohibitions against marrying the idolatrous Gentiles. And so, the people of Israel vowed to divorce their pagan wives and to walk henceforth in the law of Moses.

MY MESSENGER

The vast chronicle of the Old Testament ends with the small book of the man God called Malachi ("My Messenger").

Malachi ministered to a people in some confusion. They had undertaken their worship as in the olden days, but it was now formal and insincere. It seemed that the Hebrew nation, so thoroughly shocked over the dispersions of the Jews by Assyria and Babylon, never could regain independent footing in the Holy Land. They were controlled by Gentile thrones from afar off, heavily taxed, and always under the whims of pagan Kings. They may have kept their law out of dread fear, and their joyless existence in the Persian province of Israel was certainly nothing like the greater days under David and Solomon.

Malachi saw that the people lacked confidence and moral fiber, and he urged the priests and the populace to sincerity of worship and the steady anticipation of the coming of the promised Messiah. He assured the Chosen People of the love of God for Israel. He rebuked their sins, and he prophesied with great force about the first and second advents of the Promised One who would someday deliver Israel from every sort of bondage. He indicated that the Messiah would be preceded by the return of Elijah, the Prophet, who had, of course, been translated to heaven.

The final chapter of Malachi, and thus the final revelation of the entire Old Testament, contains a mere six verses, which provide a wholly integrated sermon on the unrepentant human condition and the Messianic solution. The coming of the Messiah, the ultimate triumph of the righteous, and the awesome power of Jehovah are given emphatically in this final message:

For, behold, the day cometh, that shall burn as an oven; and all the proud, yea, and all that do wickedly, shall be stubble: and the day that cometh shall burn them up, saith the Lord of hosts, that it shall leave them neither root nor branch.

But unto you that fear my name shall the Sun of righteousness arise with healing in his wings; and ye shall go forth, and grow up as calves of the stall.

And ye shall tread down the wicked; for they shall be ashes under the soles of your feet in the day that I shall do this, saith the Lord of hosts.

Remember ye the law of Moses my servant, which I commanded unto him in Horeb for all Israel, with the statutes and judgments.

Behold, I will send you Elijah the prophet before the coming of the great and dreadful day of the Lord:

And he shall turn the heart of the fathers to the children, and the heart of the children to their fathers, lest I come and smite the earth with a curse. (Mal. 4)

PART TWO

THE LEADING CHARACTER
AND THE HIDDEN PLOT

. . . for the testimony of Jesus is the spirit of prophecy. (Rev. 19:10)

Now all these things happened unto them for ensamples: and they are written for our admonition, upon whom the ends of the world are come. (I Cor. 10:11)

1

The Seed:
In the Beginning

Very early in the Bible, much earlier than most readers perceive, God promised the Messiah.

In fact, God promised this Deliverer just as soon as man needed a Deliverer, and that was very soon after creation indeed. By the third chapter of Genesis man desperately needed help.

Adam and Eve had not yet left Eden when the concept of a Savior Messiah was implanted into their hearts by God. Immediately after the Almighty dealt with his errant children concerning their initial sin, He turned to the serpent. The statement of God to the treacherous tempter of the Garden is almost in a different language than His conversations with Adam and Eve. Addressing the serpent, God becomes cryptic:

And I will put enmity between thee and the woman, and between thy seed and her seed; it shall bruise thy head, and thou shalt bruise his heel. (Gen. 3:15)

A very obtuse statement, in very odd terms, considering that God had previously made Himself so plain to the man and woman. But the serpent, Satan, had been dealing with God a long time; he well knew the devastating implications of this statement. It is not clear how much the distraught human couple understood at this point, but our feeling is that they perceived much of the meaning and anticipated the fulfillment.

Today, though, with the advantage of hindsight, ordinary human beings can perceive the fullness of God's subtle curse upon the devil. Essentially, the prediction indicates that there would be a state of war between humanity and Satan. Into this struggle would ultimately come the Seed of the Woman, who would enter into battle with Satan. The Seed of the Woman would sustain a minor, temporary injury, like a bruise of the heel, but Satan's head would be dealt a mortal blow.

The term "Seed of the Woman" is curious. Elsewhere in the Bible the "seed" is seen as of the man (like "the seed of Abraham"), and indeed it is the male who provides the seed, in terms of conception. Is it possible that our first mother, Eve, perceived from God's statement that the promised Seed would come from a woman alone—a virgin birth?

In any case, with this remarkable statement God planted in the human heart the hope of a miraculous coming Satan-Destroyer, who would battle the devil and avenge the lie of the serpent and its devastating results.

FOLLOWING THE SEED

The question naturally arose, assuming that Adam and Eve perceived the meaning of God's promise of the Seed, as to where the Seed might come from. What would be his family and national origin?

Our first parents might well have assumed that the seed promise would be accomplished through the line of Abel, their more faithful son, but Cain murdered him before Abel had a child. Adam and Eve had another son, then, specifically to replace Abel ("For God, said she, hath appointed me another seed instead of Abel, whom Cain slew").

It was Seth, the new son, who would provide the Messianic line now, rather than Cain, whose line was more rebellious. The promise of God would be carried through by the later child.

Following the line of Seth in the Biblical genealogies is discouraging, however. After a millennium or so it is clear that the line of Seth has become almost completely corrupted. Only Noah, as we saw in Part One, found grace in the eyes of the Lord.

Noah had three sons of varying allegiance to God, and after the Flood he singled out Shem as the one most directly related to the Lord. *Shem*, in fact, means "the Name," and evidences the close relationship of this particular personality with the name of Yahweh, the Lord. The "Shemitic," or Semitic, races all descended from Shem and all of the information the world has about God comes from them.

So the Seed promise descends, thus far, through Seth and Shem. The concept is to become more clear and more intense as the Old Testament unfolds.

With Abraham, about a thousand years later, the Seed promise becomes very definite and specific. Messianic prophecy begins in earnest with God's friend from Ur:

And in thy seed shall all the nations of the earth be blessed; because thou hast obeyed my voice. (Gen. 22:18)

In addition to the Seed promise, God made a covenant with Abraham which granted him a land and a royal dynasty:

Arise, walk through the land in the length of it and in the breadth of it; for I will give it unto thee. (Gen. 13:17)

And I will make thee exceeding fruitful, and I will make nations of thee, and kings shall come out of thee. (Gen. 17:6)

The remarkable passage Genesis 12:1–3 actually gives the whole of the Abrahamic Covenant in one statement, true to God's usual style. Abraham, the Mesopotamian, must have been overwhelmed. It is easier for us today, having seen the results of God's promises, to appreciate the fullness of His generosity. Abraham, seemingly selected at random, was the patriarch in whom Messianic prophecy crystallized.

The land, of course, was against the Mediterranean coast in the area that came to be known as Palestine and then Israel, out of which came the Messiah. *The seed* is now seen to be Abraham's descendants: In the broadest sense, all of his descendants, including the Arab nations and also those who believe in God as Abraham did; in a narrower sense to the nation Israel, Abraham's direct descendants; and finally in the most specific sense to the Messiah, in whom all the nations of the earth are blessed (Gen. 22:17). *The royal dynasty* was realized in Abraham's descendant

King David, and in David's greater Son, the Messiah, the King of Kings.

It is clear that Abraham understood the promises and he appealed to God, at the point where he had just one son, that the promises go through Ishmael. But it was God's choice that the covenant, and the Seed promise in particular, should come down through Isaac. Ishmael, the father of the Arab nations, was also to be honored (Gen. 21:12) but the covenant proceeds through Isaac and his line.

Isaac had two sons, Jacob and Esau, and God again made a choice, electing to continue the Seed promise through Jacob:

> . . . I am the Lord God of Abraham thy father, and the God of Isaac: the land whereon thou liest, to thee will I give it, and to thy seed; . . . and in thee [Jacob] and in thy seed shall all the families of the earth be blessed. (Gen. 28:13–14)

And so there was a constant process of selection narrowing the Messianic line from Shem, through Abraham, Isaac, and Jacob. It is rather like a vast elimination contest in which men observe each single step but God knows the outcome. Complete charts have been drawn, with the help of the Biblical genealogies, illustrating the exact progression of the Messianic promise from creation to the very birth of Jesus.

Jacob had twelve sons but God still made His individual choice. Near the end of Jacob's long life the patriarch spoke prophecies about each of his sons, and when we come to his forecast for Judah's line the message is clear:

> The sceptre shall not depart from Judah, nor a lawgiver from between his feet, until Shiloh come; and unto him shall the gathering of the people be. (Gen. 49:10)

The scepter, the symbol of royalty, expresses the kingly prerogatives of the Messiah. David, and Jesus after him, came out of the Tribe of Judah.

Direct revelation about the Messiah then ceases for hundreds of years, during the period of Israel's enslavement in Egypt. But after the Exodus, during the forty years of wandering in the wilderness, God speaks of the Messiah again, and in a curious way. The heathen prophet Baalim declares:

> I shall see him, but not now: I shall behold him, but not nigh: there shall come a Star out of Jacob, and a Sceptre shall rise out of Israel, and shall smite the corners of Moab, and destroy all the children of Sheth. (Num. 24:17)

The royal power (Star and Scepter) of the coming Messiah is emphasized in this prophecy, and His ability to overcome all the enemies of the Lord and Israel. It is clear to the non-Israelite Baal that the great ruler he speaks of will come out of Israel.

The last definitive Messianic prophecy in the Pentateuch is found in one of Moses' final addresses before the Hebrew nation previous to their entering the Promised Land:

> I will raise them up a Prophet from among their brethren, like unto thee, and will put my words in his mouth; and he shall speak unto them all that I shall command him.

> And it shall come to pass, that whosoever will not hearken unto my words which he shall speak in my name, I will require it of him. (Deut. 18:18-19)

This is new information. The Messiah, it is now seen, will be a prophet, much the same as Moses. In addition to being a Satan-Destroyer and King with enormous divine power, he will also teach and speak the Word of God, as did Moses. And further, God will require everyone to listen to this prophet; if anyone refuses to hear Him, that person will be judged.

Thus, in the first five books of the Bible, God progresses from His subtle announcement that the Seed of the Woman will crush the head of the Serpent to details of the character of the Messiah. The Messianic line is narrowed steadily through Seth, Shem, Abraham, Isaac, Jacob, and Judah. The Messiah will have royal power and He will be a prophet like Moses, God concludes in this section of the Bible.

Much more revelation about the Messiah continues through the Old Testament as God, through prophecy and ongoing promises about the great hope of Israel and the world, establishes intimate details about the coming King.

2

The Promise:
The King Is Coming

After the subtle revelations of the Pentateuch concerning the Seed promises, information about the Messiah takes on the force of direct prophecy. As the Old Testament progresses, we gather more and more information about the Promised One, until it is extremely clear just who He is, when He comes, and what His mission concerns.

The final information about the Seed in the Pentateuch concerned the royal Tribe of Judah, but it was some eight hundred years later before a descendant of Judah actually became King over Israel. With the anointing of Jesse's son, David, "a man after God's own heart" (I Sam. 16:13), the scepter arrives at Judah and then never departs.

We have seen that David's son Solomon built the Temple of God in Jerusalem, and that God promised that David's house, or dynasty, would endure forever (II Sam. 7:4–17).

It might be questioned as to whether the dynasty of the House of David of Judah has survived, but the Lord supplied later, through the prophet Jeremiah, that He certainly meant to fulfill this promise:

Thus saith the Lord; If ye can break my covenant of the day, and my covenant of the night, and that there should not be day and night in their season;

Then may also my covenant be broken with David my servant, that he should not have a son to reign upon his throne; and with the Levites the priests, my ministers.

As the host of heaven cannot be numbered, neither the sand of the sea measured: so will I multiply the seed of David my servant, and the Levites that minister unto me. (Jer. 33:20–22)

Understanding in advance that Israel would go into captivity, and that the line of the reign of Kings would become confused, the Lord reassured readers of prophecy that the promises to David were immutable. As surely as night follows day, the Lord will ultimately establish the throne of David forever:

Thus saith the Lord; If my covenant be not with day and night, and if I have not appointed the ordinances of heaven and earth;

Then will I cast away the seed of Jacob, and David my servant, so that I will not take any of his seed to be rulers over the seed of Abraham, Isaac, and Jacob: for I will cause their captivity to return, and have mercy on them. (Jer. 33:25–26)

Of course, the Davidic monarchy ceased after the Babylonian captivity, but meticulous genealogical records were kept for centuries in the Temple archives. Tribal members were listed with their correct tribes, and the writers of the New Testament gospels are most careful to point out that Jesus Christ is a lineal descendant of David, both through the line of his mother, Mary, and his foster father, Joseph. If circumstances had permitted the line of Judah to keep the throne through the millennium from David to Christ, then Joseph, the Nazarene carpenter, would have been the rightful King of Israel. But, in any case, instead, the Messiah, the "Son of David" (Matthew 1:1), was born into the humble home of Joseph and thus obtained the legal right to the throne, which still remained in the Davidic line. Thus, God's promise to David of an eternal dynasty is wonderfully fulfilled by the eternal Messiah being born in the very family of David, and becoming the true heir to the throne of Israel. The Romans most accurately identified the crucified Messiah as "The King of the Jews."

And of necessity, Jesus is the final King of the line of David; all the Temple records and genealogies were destroyed by the Romans in the siege of A.D. 70, when the Second Temple was vanquished. Thus, no other person born since that time can prove he was a descendant of David. All the lines of the Davidic dynasty focus on Jesus and terminate in Him. He is now, spiritually speaking, the reigning King of the Jews, and, as the Old Testament prophets tell us, will return to occupy the throne of David in the kingdom to come (Ezek. 37:24–25, et al.).

UNTO US A CHILD IS BORN

As the Old Testament record progresses, very decisive prophecies about the Messiah appear. Some three hundred years after David, the prophet Micah received the revelation that the Messiah would be born in the same little village where David himself was born. Bethlehem, about five miles south of Jerusalem, was to receive this singular honor:

> But thou, Bethlehem Ephratah, though thou be little among the thousands of Judah, yet out of thee shall he come forth unto me that is to be ruler in Israel; whose goings forth have been from of old, from everlasting. (Mic. 5:2)

This minor prophet, a contemporary of the great Isaiah, looks down the corridor of the future, seeing that one of the smallest towns in Judah would be thus glorified.

When the time came for the fulfillment of this prophecy, it took some doing. The true heir to David's throne, Joseph of Nazareth, lived with his wife, Mary, in northern Israel nearly a hundred miles from Bethlehem. Mary was with child and undoubtedly planned to give birth in Nazareth, but the Lord put it in the heart of Caesar Augustus, who bore the grand title "The Emperor of the World," to conduct a "worldwide" census for tax purposes. All Israelites had to register for the census in their ancestral cities at that precise time. Joseph was obliged to journey to Bethlehem, the ancestral origin of the Davidic family. He couldn't very well leave the pregnant Mary in Nazareth, and so they undertook together the troublesome journey over mountainous terrain, with Mary on the verge of giving birth. They made it, barely, unable to find a room at the inn in little Bethlehem, and the Messiah was born in a manger in the city of His fathers.

And as to that birth, it was, of course, a very special one. There had been a number of births attended by divine dispensations in the Scriptures, such as those of Isaac and Samuel. But in the case of the Messiah, there was to be a virgin birth! This remarkable prediction was made by Isaiah to King Ahaz of Judah around 730 B.C.

It was a desperate time for Jerusalem when this singular prophecy was spoken. The Holy City was undergoing a siege by the united armies of strange bedfellows—Israel, the northern kingdom, and Syria. The two unlikely allies were determined to overthrow Ahaz and install a puppet king over Judah. The King and the people of the Holy City were shaking like the leaves of the forest (Isa. 7:2).

Isaiah met with Ahaz as the King was inspecting the defenses and water supply on the city wall, and assured the sovereign that Israel and Syria would not harm Judah, and that, as a matter of fact, within sixty-five years the northern kingdom of Israel would be broken (Isa. 7:7-8). This prophecy correctly identified the Assyrian destruction of both Syria and Israel.

Then, Isaiah challenged Ahaz to ask for some great sign from the Lord to confirm His promise of deliverance. It could be anything in heaven and earth—the sky was the limit for this sign. Ahaz, not a particularly God-fearing King, was unimpressed. He was one of the most idolatrous and evil of Judah's Kings (II Kings 16:3). He had offered his own son in a pagan sacrificial rite, at one point. But, in mock piety, he answered the respected prophet that he would "not ask, neither will I test the Lord" (Isa. 7:12).

The patient Isaiah declared that the Lord Himself would give Ahaz a magnificent sign, whether he wanted one or not. A virgin would conceive and bear a son, whose name would be Immanuel —meaning "God with us" ("Therefore the Lord Himself shall give you a sign; Behold, a virgin shall conceive, and bear a son, and shall call his name Immanuel"; Isa. 7:14).

It was some seven centuries before that prophecy was fulfilled by the birth of Christ of the Virgin Mary, of course, but Isaiah also supplied the skeptical Ahaz with a sign that he would live to see fulfilled. Isaiah himself had an infant son and he assured the King that before that boy would be able to cry "Mommy" or "Daddy," Syria and Israel would be ransacked by Assyria (Isa.

8:1–4). And that event came to pass as surely as did the Messianic prophecy.

Thus, there was a prophecy concerning Isaiah's own son which came to pass immediately, intensifying the more distant sign of the virgin-born Immanuel.

Isaiah rose to truly magnificent heights in his glorious description of the coming Messiah in an oft quoted passage:

> For unto us a child is born, unto us a son is given: and the government shall be upon his shoulder: and his name shall be called Wonderful, Counsellor, The mighty God, The everlasting Father, The Prince of Peace.
>
> Of the increase of his government and peace there shall be no end, upon the throne of David, and upon his kingdom, to order it, and to establish it with judgment and with justice from henceforth even for ever. The zeal of the Lord of hosts will perform this. (Isa. 9:6–7)

THE SUFFERING LAMB

But a second aspect, apparently contradictory, begins to appear about the Promised One of God. He is Messiah, yes; King, yes; Lord of all, yes. But, oddly, He is also to suffer and die. How can the two kinds of prophecies exist side by side?

Isaiah gives one of the most compelling descriptions of the Suffering Servant of the Lord in his incomparable fifty-second and fifty-third chapters. Beginning with the exaltation of God's servant as being of the highest spiritual order, Isaiah then describes the Messiah as becoming marred and disfigured—even astonishing to look at—yet He would sprinkle many nations and thus purify and cleanse them. The Gentile nations, who had no prophecy about the Messiah, would still come to Him, Isaiah says:

> So shall he sprinkle many nations; the kings shall shut their mouths at him: for that which had not been told them shall they see; and that which they had not heard shall they consider. (Isa. 52:15)

Unfortunately, regrets Isaiah, not a great many will believe his message about the Servant. The prophet asks, "Who hath believed our report?"

The drama of Isa. 53 is so clear and so illustrative of the earthly ministry of Jesus that we reprint it in full here:

Who hath believed our report? and to whom is the arm of the Lord revealed?

For he shall grow up before him as a tender plant, and as a root out of a dry ground: he hath no form nor comeliness; and when we shall see him, there is no beauty that we should desire him.

He is despised and rejected of men; a man of sorrows, and acquainted with grief: and we hid as it were our faces from him; he was despised, and we esteemed him not.

Surely he hath borne our griefs, and carried our sorrows: yet we did esteem him stricken, smitten of God, and afflicted.

But he was wounded for our transgressions, he was bruised for our iniquities: the chastisement of our peace was upon him; and with his stripes we are healed.

All we like sheep have gone astray; we have turned every one to his own way; and the Lord hath laid on him the iniquity of us all.

He was oppressed, and he was afflicted, yet he opened not his mouth: he is brought as a lamb to the slaughter, and as a sheep before her shearers is dumb, so he openeth not his mouth.

He was taken from prison and from judgment: and who shall declare his generation? for he was cut off out of the land of the living: for the transgression of my people was he stricken.

And he made his grave with the wicked, and with the rich in his death; because he had done no violence, neither was any deceit in his mouth.

Yet it pleased the Lord to bruise him; he hath put him to grief: when thou shalt make his soul an offering for sin, he shall see his seed, he shall prolong his days, and the pleasure of the Lord shall prosper in his hand.

He shall see of the travail of his soul, and shall be satisfied: by his knowledge shall my righteous servant justify many; for he shall bear their iniquities.

Therefore will I divide him a portion with the great, and he shall divide the spoil with the strong; because he hath poured out his soul unto death: and he was numbered with the transgressors; and he bare the sin of many, and made intercession for the transgressors. (Isa. 53)

Thus, the intercessory mission of the Messiah is made clear, the circumstances of His trial, and the details of His death and burial.

The Lord would consider His Servant's death as an offering for sin, and would "prolong His days," and "see His seed even after death." His Servant would have an enormous reward, because in His death He took upon Himself the sins of many.

It is the Christian position, of course, to render such prophecies as pertaining directly to Jesus Christ, and they are obviously difficult to assign otherwise. Jesus was the Servant of God who became a man, but was terribly marred during His judgment by the tearing out of His beard, the crown of thorns, and the flogging. He did come of humble origins, "as a root out of dry ground," and He was rejected. He died a substitutionary death for our sins, according to the gospels. He did not raise any defense for Himself in either His Israeli or Roman trial; He remained silent, "as a sheep before her shearers is dumb, so he openeth not his mouth." He was crucified with the wicked—two thieves—and Joseph of Arimathaea, a rich man, buried the body in his own stone sepulcher. He "prolonged his days" by rising from the dead, and is seeing His seed in the multitudes who believe in Him as Savior. His reward will be fully obtained when He returns to establish His worldwide kingdom and when He rules the new Jerusalem forever.

The Isaiah passage quoted above is perhaps the fullest and most detailed description of the ministry of the Messiah to be found in the Old Testament.

While Isaiah's writings are replete with such references to the coming Promised One, King David as well spoke of Him, supplying the fact that the Messiah would, indeed, be resurrected after His earthly death. If Isaiah is the prophet of the death of the Messiah, then King David is the prophet of His resurrection.

In the definitive sixteenth Psalm, David spoke of the Holy One, one of the many titles of the Messiah given in the Old Testament. He described Him at the point when His soul had gone to Sheol (the dwelling of the dead during Old Testament times) and His body had been entombed. In other words, the Holy One has died physically. David then prophesied that the Holy One's flesh will rest "in hope" because God would not leave His soul in Sheol and His entombed body would not see decay.

David's passage was quoted by the apostles Peter and Paul with great effect to show that Jesus Christ fulfilled the prophecy when He arose from the tomb the third day after He died. As David had originally prophesied:

> Therefore my heart is glad, and my glory rejoiceth: my flesh also shall rest in hope.

> For thou wilt not leave my soul in hell; neither wilt thou suffer thine Holy One to see corruption.

> Thou wilt shew me the path of life: in thy presence *is* fulness of joy; at thy right hand *there are* pleasures for evermore. (Ps. 16:9–11)

Jesus, of course, rose from the tomb, conquering death and the grave, and was truly shown the path of life in His resurrection power. The apostles' message, with reference to the Psalm of David, resulted in thousands of conversions in the New Testament times (Acts 2:25–32; 13:35–37).

"THY KINGDOM COME"

It is sometimes not appreciated that the Old Testament contains prophecy not only about the initial coming of the Messiah, but about His second advent, as well. It does not merely picture Christ's atoning death and resurrection, but also His return in glory.

We have seen that the prophets Joel, Zechariah, Ezekiel, and others, accurately depicted the "end times," or "latter days" (Jer. 37).

These latter days, which have not arrived as yet in the course of human events, will be a time of dreadful persecution for the Jewish people—certainly no strangers to persecution. The pain will be so great that strong men will double over in agony like women in labor, the record states. Terrible power will emerge in a False Messiah, described as a "Wicked Prince," who will deceive the world with illusions and tremendous political strength (Jer. 36; Dan. 8:23–26).

Finally, all the nations and armed forces of the world will encircle and invade the small country of Israel, and will seek to destroy the Holy Land and Jerusalem once and for all. The warfare will be all-encompassing and it will appear that Israel is lost. Half the City of Jerusalem will be captured and annihilated. This will be the nation of Israel's darkest and most distressing hour, in her long, long history of distressing hours:

> And in that day will I make Jerusalem a burdensome stone for all people: all that burden themselves with it shall be cut in pieces, though all the people of the earth be gathered together against it. (Zech. 12:3)

However, this time of tribulation will also mark the return of the Messiah. He will arrive at the Mount of Olives overlooking the east side of Jerusalem, from where He ascended to His Father after the resurrection:

> And his feet shall stand in that day upon the mount of Olives, which is before Jerusalem on the east, and the mount of Olives shall cleave in the midst thereof toward the east and toward the west, and there shall be a very great valley; and half of the mountain shall remove toward the north, and half of it toward the south. (Zech. 14:4)

He will miraculously deliver the Jewish people from the terrible Armageddon. The Israeli generals will become like "God," and the ordinary soldiers will be like King David in their ferocious repulsion of the invading armies. The Lord will fight for them and will rout their enemies:

> In that day shall the Lord defend the inhabitants of Jerusalem; and he that is feeble among them at that day shall be as David; and the house of David shall be as God, as the angel of the Lord before them.
>
> And it shall come to pass in that day, that I will seek to destroy all the nations that come against Jerusalem. (Zech. 12:8–9)

The moment will mark a deeply moving spiritual regeneration of the people of Israel. When the Messiah arrives, they will "look upon Him whom they have pierced," "and mourn for Him":

> And I will pour upon the house of David, and upon the inhabitants of Jerusalem, the spirit of grace and of supplications: and they shall look upon me whom they have pierced, and they shall mourn for him, as one mourneth for his only son, and shall be in bitterness for him, as one that is in bitterness for his firstborn. (Zech. 12:10)
>
> In that day there shall be a fountain opened to the house of David and to the inhabitants of Jerusalem for sin and for uncleanness. (Zech. 13:1)

The entirety of the Jewish nation that has endured to that time will realize that the One that they did not recognize as their Messiah in His first advent—the One they had pierced for supposed blasphemy—is indeed their own Delivering Messiah. The rescue will be complete, as the Lord finally sanctifies Israel nationally and spiritually (Rom. 11:26).

Jesus Christ taught His disciples that He was, in fact, the Messiah, and that after He died and rose from the dead and ascended into Heaven, He would be gone for a time (John 14:1–3). But He assured them that He would return to fulfill the rest of the prophecies.

We realize, of course, that the disciples had only the Old Testament prophecies to depend on, but the Lord still assured them that they would all be fulfilled—including the prophecies of the second coming. The Lord predicted that at His return, Israel would welcome Him, saying, "Blessed is he that cometh in the name of the Lord" (Matt. 23:39).

The New Testament adds many details to this "time of Jacob's trouble," just preceding the return of Christ, and it agrees perfectly with the Old Testament revelations. Here again, in prophecies written centuries and even millennia apart by different authors of different times and persuasions, we see a cohesive picture of a dramatic coming event in both Testaments. The return of Christ is, of course, the great hope of Christianity and the spiritual factor that sets it apart from all other religions. The Jewish people today, by and large, do not accept Jesus Christ as the Messiah, although some of them do await a coming Messiah in accordance with the Old Testament revelations. Zechariah discloses, then, that when Jesus returns, the Jewish people as well as the rest of the world will be completely informed as to who He was and is.

Thus will the kingdom of the Lord at last come to the earth, and His Will shall be "done in earth as it is in heaven." After more than four thousand years of primarily discouraging history, Israel will enter a glorious golden age of peace, prosperity, and spiritual vitality. All believers will join together, Jew and Gentile, under the true Messiah's wise rule. There will be genuine justice and political equality in Israel and throughout the world:

And there shall come forth a rod out of the stem of Jesse, and a Branch shall grow out of his roots:

And the spirit of the Lord shall rest upon him, the spirit of wisdom and understanding, the spirit of counsel and might, the spirit of knowledge and of the fear of the Lord;

And shall make him of quick understanding in the fear of the Lord: and He shall not judge after the sight of his eyes, neither reprove after the hearing of his ears:

But with righteousness shall he judge the poor, and reprove with equity for the meek of the earth: and he shall smite the earth with the rod of his mouth, and with the breath of his lips shall he slay the wicked.

And righteousness shall be the girdle of his loins, and faithfulness the girdle of his reins. (Isa. 11:1–5)

Uniquely, the Old Testament is much more descriptive concerning the kingdom reign of the Lord after His second coming, than is the New Testament. Isaiah, particularly, gives idyllic scenes of peace and tranquillity:

The wolf also shall dwell with the lamb, and the leopard shall lie down with the kid; and the calf and the young lion and the fatling together; and a little child shall lead them.

And the cow and the bear shall feed; their young ones shall lie down together: and the lion shall eat straw like the ox.

And the sucking child shall play on the hole of the asp, and the weaned child shall put his hand on the cockatrice' den.

They shall not hurt nor destroy in all my holy mountain: for the earth shall be full of the knowledge of the Lord, as the waters cover the sea. (Isa. 11:6–9)

Israel, the Promised Land, will become the head of the nations in the Kingdom Age, and Jerusalem will be the acknowledged theocratic, political, and religious capital of the world. Every nation will send representatives to Jerusalem to learn the ways of the Lord who reigns there:

And it shall come to pass in the last days, that the mountain of the Lord's house shall be established in the top of the mountains, and shall be exalted above the hills; and all nations shall flow unto it.

And many people shall go and say, Come ye, and let us go up to the mountain of the Lord, to the house of the God of Jacob; and he will teach us of his ways, and we will walk in his paths: for out of Zion shall go forth the law, and the word of the Lord from Jerusalem.

And he shall judge among the nations, and shall rebuke many people: and they shall beat their swords into plowshares, and their spears into pruninghooks: nation shall not lift up sword against nation, neither shall they learn war any more. (Isa. 2:2–4)

Again, Jesus Christ stated that He would fulfill these particular prophecies. He promised His twelve disciples that they would rule over the twelve tribes of Israel in His future kingdom (Matt. 19:28).

JESUS IN THE OLD TESTAMENT

Thus, we see that Jesus Christ is, indeed, the leading character of the Old Testament. His identity is gradually and carefully developed in the "Seed promises" of the Pentateuch, and major aspects of His first and second advents are prophesied throughout the rest of the Old Testament revelation.

There are, of course, many more prophecies that might be mentioned in connection with the details of the Lord's two advents, but we have tried to illustrate the major ones in this space. Some Bible analysts have counted over three hundred prophecies directly referring to Jesus and giving highly detailed references to the events of His ministry. But some of the prophecies are merely brief mentions, which take the form of Bible "types," or symbols, rather than spun-out explanations. In our next section, we are going to deal with these Biblical symbols, which illustrate the true, almost hidden, plot of the Old Testament.

It is interesting to Bible readers to contemplate where we stand now in the progress of God's plan for redemption. We have seen the first advent of the Messiah, if the prophets are to be believed, and we have not, as yet, seen the second. The coming of the "latter days" of tribulation for Israel and the world are the hallmark of the return of the Messiah, and many prophecy analysts today feel that a remarkable number of characteristics of those terrible times are presently identifiable. Naturally, people have claimed throughout the ages that the return of the Lord was imminent, but it does seem reasonable, from a strictly Biblical point of view, that certain characteristics of the present times line up well with the Biblical descriptions of the tribulation preceding the Kingdom age.

For one thing, the nation of Israel has been restored, as of 1948, and the Hebrew people have once again controlled the Holy City,

Jerusalem, since the 1967 war. These two pieces of the prophetic puzzle certainly had to be in place before any of the above prophecies could progress. Then we have the development of world animosity toward Israel, an unfortunate but important constituent of end times prophecy which we could not have pointed out even five years ago. The Middle East power struggle, an issue since the times of Joshua, has intensified lately so that it is hardly a local matter. The entire world is concerned, due to the oil crisis and the interests of the major powers in the situation surrounding Israel and her neighbors today.

Peculiarly, the Bible seems to have come of age. Over the past few centuries it has been, of course, the respected Holy Book of all Christendom, and Judaism as well, but more recently it has captured the interest of even secular analysts of our future. In its uncanny way, the Bible gives those clear-eyed forecasts that seem to agree so well with developing situations, and this has come to the attention of open-minded readers.

But, to go back to our subject—the Leading Character of the Old Testament—we can see that the Bible, of necessity, gives the circumstances of the two comings of the Messiah. It was imperative for men to recognize the first advent of the Lord in order that they obtain salvation through Him and be reconciled to God. It is doubly imperative that they recognize the second, since, putting it very simply, there will be no further chances.

The entire Old Testament revelation, then, hinges on the vital importance and saving mission of a single human being—Jesus Christ.

3

Buried Treasures:
Shadows of Christ

The cryptic types, or illustrations of the Messiah, that are found throughout the Old Testament make its study a rewarding and refreshing experience for those who believe in the Messiah and the fulfillment of the New Testament. Truly, there is more to the saga of the Old Testament than meets the eye; there is a hidden plot, in pictures and symbols.

There are types in the Old Testament that portray almost every teaching in the New Testament. Authentic types may be found for the entire panorama of the Messianic program; the death and resurrection of Christ, the second advent of the Lord, the age of the Church, the believer's life in the Lord, and the future of Israel and the world.

To help define the term "type," we might give one of the obvious Old Testament examples at this point. Paramount in the Old Testament chronology is, of course, the deliverance of the Hebrews out of Egypt, accomplished by means of the blood of the lamb. As we related above, the Lord delivered the Israelites by having them place the blood of the lamb on their doorposts; when the avenging angel saw the blood, he passed over the homes of the Israelites during the awesome tenth plague. The entire Passover drama presents a beautiful allegory to the New Testament situation of the blood of Christ delivering the believer out of the slavery to sin. Egypt is a type of the world in all its paganism; the Israelites, a type of God's People; the blood of the lamb is a type of the sacrifice which reconciles the people to God, and finally, the deliverance to the Promised Land is a type of the believer going to heaven. Jesus is referred to throughout the Old Testament as "the Lamb," and by John the Baptist as "the Lamb of God, which taketh away the sin of the world" (John 1:29). Thus, we see the full meaning of this beautiful type: in any age, the believer, whether Old Testament Jew or New Testament Christian, can rely on the fact that "the blood of the Lamb delivers me from bondage." The fact that Jesus, the Lamb of God, was crucified precisely on the day of Passover clinches the type.

We will review below a number of the more important types in the Old Testament, but the reader should be aware that this is a profound study in itself. There are hundreds, perhaps thousands, of subtle symbols and illustrations throughout the Old Testament writing, and Biblical analysts are continually uncovering new ones. The entire system of the hidden plot—the arrangement of types, symbols, and illustrations well before their fulfillments in time—certainly underlines the evidence that the Old Testament is the writing of the Lord. Certainly, no ordinary men, however intelligent or spiritual, could have written such pointed and subtle symbolism about events that had not yet occurred.

THE SEVEN FEASTS AND THE MESSIANIC SYSTEM

Since we began with the illustration of the beautiful type of Passover, we might now continue with the other Old Testament feasts and show how they portray later developments in the New Testament and even in our own future.

When the Lord gave the Law to Israel on Mount Sinai, He included with it an annual calendar of events which He called "the feasts of the Lord." These seven feasts, beginning with Passover in the spring, and ending with Tabernacles in the fall, comprise a wonderful picture of the panorama of God's entire prophetic program. They speak of the Messiah, including His death, burial, and resurrection, His sending of the Holy Spirit for the Church, His second coming, the redemption of Israel, and the establishment of God's kingdom on the earth. The feasts, taken together, represent undoubtedly the most comprehensive of all of the Old Testament types. The Jewish people continue to keep their feasts today in somewhat altered forms, little realizing that the rituals of the worship they perform teach great truths about Jesus Christ.

It is difficult to summarize so complete a lesson in prophecy as the feasts present. They are given in a single Biblical chapter, Lev. 23, with their dates and the high points of the observance for each. The prophetic issues which they symbolize can be explained easily from the New Testament and from the further prophecy throughout the Bible.

Passover is first, as we said, and represents redemption by the blood of the Lamb. The second feast, Unleavened Bread, beginning the next evening, represents the body of the Lord ("This bread is my body"; "I am the bread of life"). The third feast is First Fruits—now called Easter—and occurs on the Sunday after Passover. It symbolizes the early spring crops, the first fruits out of the ground, as it were, and, in type, it symbolizes the resurrection of Jesus Christ, the first man "out of the ground," that is, permanently resurrected. Interestingly, the Lord commemorated each of these feasts in an especially appropriate way at the termination of His earthly ministry. He was crucified on the day of Passover, buried on the beginning day of Unleavened Bread, and resurrected on the day of First Fruits.

We would expect, then, that the fourth feast would symbolize the next important act of the Lord, and indeed it does. The harvest feast of Pentecost, to be observed fifty days after First Fruits, marks the coming of the Holy Spirit and the birth of the Christian Church (Acts 2), quite a harvest. The fifth feast, the feast of Trumpets, has not been fulfilled, as yet; prophecy tells us, however, that the return of the Lord for the Church will be accompanied by the sound of trumpets (I Thess. 4:16–17; I Cor. 15:51–53). Thus, while the Lord may come at any moment, He may reasonably be expected to return for the Church on some future feast of Trumpets (occurring in late summer or early fall), if He chooses to remain consistent with the schedule of the feasts. The Day of Atonement is the sixth feast, and will mark the return of the Lord to the earth for the beginning of the kingdom. We saw in the prophecy of Zechariah how Israel would "mourn for Him," and "look upon Him whom they have pierced." This future day of atonement will result in Israel's ultimate salvation. Finally, the seventh feast, Tabernacles, obviously symbolizes the Kingdom Age on earth, when the Lord's Tabernacle will be established in Jerusalem for annual worship on the part of all nations (Zech. 14:16–19; Ezek. 37:27–28).

Thus, the order of the feasts and the nature of each one of them give a glimpse ahead at God's entire Messianic plan. They tell the story of redemption from the initial blood of the Lamb to the establishment of the reign of the Messiah on earth.*

ADAM AND CHRIST

Adam, the first human being, is a type of Christ in the sense that through one grand act he affected the Almighty's ultimate plans for life and death.

Adam is the head, the founder, the origin of the natural physical human race, while Christ is the head of a new human race— the redeemed human beings. When Adam disobeyed God, he died, and passed on this disease of physical and spiritual death to all of his children. This is the meaning of the doctrine of "original sin"—we are all children of Adam, and thus born in sin apart from God. Adam's one sin was passed down to every one of us. We know that this is true, because we still obtain the same result from the symptoms that Adam had; we die. Physical death is the obvious proof that we have inherited Adam's tendency to sin. "The wages of sin is death."

But in Christ, death has been conquered. Through Christ's magnificent act of obedience to God in His sacrificial death, He in effect canceled the punishment that Adam had fallen into. His atonement passes on to those who believe in Him, and they are granted eternal life. Just as Adam's legacy was death, Christ's legacy is eternal life for all believers (Rom. 5:12–21; I Cor. 15:22–23).

Thus, those believing in the Lord Jesus Christ receive eternal life and become members of His new redeemed race of mankind. That, in essence, is the Christian faith.

* For a more complete discussion of the feasts in all of their subtle meanings, see *Raptured*, by the authors, Harvest House, 1975.

FATHERS AND SONS

Abraham and Isaac present a picture of God the Father and His Son, Jesus.

Isaac was the seed, the son of promise, and was miraculously born of a mother too old to bear children. Jesus, of course, was miraculously born as well, of a virgin. When the Lord commanded Abraham to take his only son, Isaac, to Mount Moriah and offer him as a sacrifice, He was presenting a poignant picture of what He Himself would do two thousand years later when He, God Almighty, would offer up His only Son, Jesus, as a sacrifice for sin. God's offering was even made on the same mountain— Mount Moriah, the site of the Temple.

Not only is the death of Christ portrayed in this scenario, but also His resurrection. As the New Testament writer makes clear, Abraham believed that all of God's promises concerning Isaac would be fulfilled, even if Isaac died. Thus, Abraham trusted that God would raise Isaac from the dead to keep His Word (Heb. 11:7–19).

Therefore, as Isaac lived on and became the father of an entire race of Chosen People, so Christ lives on, the Father of an entire race of Chosen People.

REJECTED, THEN ACCEPTED

Joseph, the Hebrew who achieved such success in the government of Egypt, presents an interesting type of Christ as one who was first rejected, and then finally accepted, by his own brothers. When the first Jewish Christian martyr, Stephen, was stoned to death in Jerusalem in the New Testament account, he gave a thorough historical lecture on the way the Chosen People had consistently rejected the great Hebrew prophets the Lord had sent, including the Messiah Himself (Acts 7:51–52). Among Stephen's examples were Joseph and Moses.

Joseph, of course, presented himself twice to his eleven patriarchal brothers as the one ordained of God to be their leader. When he was a teenager, he told them of his dream where his brothers would bow down to him and serve him. They responded with ridicule, anger, and even hatred. They sold Joseph into slavery among the Gentiles.

But God preserved Joseph and eventually elevated him to vice-Pharaoh of Egypt. When famine then came to Canaan, the brothers appealed to the vice-Pharaoh for grain, and Joseph, at length, revealed himself to them. They then bowed down to the formerly detested brother and reunited with him.

In the very same way, Jesus of Nazareth has been rejected, to a large extent, by His Hebrew brothers. His claims to be Israel's Messiah have been spurned and ridiculed. To a large extent, He has been thrown off to the Gentiles, a number of whom have welcomed, exalted, and received the Jewish Messiah. He is, in effect, now a Ruler in the Gentile world in the manner that Joseph ruled in Egypt. It should be noticed, however, that just as Joseph's young full brother, Benjamin, remained faithful to him, so Christ has a remnant among His own Jewish people that are faithful to Him. At the second coming of the Messiah, the Jewish nation will welcome and acknowledge Him, as we saw in the prophecies.

Thus, just as Joseph was finally seen to truly be the sovereign that he claimed to be by his brothers, Jesus will eventually be accepted and honored by Israel, His brethren.

ISRAEL IN EGYPT

The entire nation of Israel itself is easily seen to be a type of Jesus the Messiah. Israel, in the patriarchal times, moved from the Promised Land to Egypt, and later, by the power of God, was brought out of Egypt and back to the land. The Lord told Moses that Israel was His first-born son among the nations, and thus He brought them out of Egypt (Ex. 4:21-23). Later, the prophet Hosea referred to God's calling of Israel out of Egypt in words that are precisely quoted in the New Testament:

When Israel was a child, then I loved him, and called my son out of Egypt. (Hos. 11:1)

Jesus Himself was obliged to endure a temporary sojourn in Egypt in his youth. The gospels tell us that shortly after His birth, Jesus was spirited away to Egypt by his parents because of King Herod's order that every infant in Bethlehem be killed. The murderous Herod wanted to eliminate any possible pretender to the throne (and this infanticide itself answers to the Egyptian infanticide to prevent the birth of Moses).

When the time of the horrible murdering was done, Joseph, Mary, and their Blessed Son returned to settle in Nazareth, and so, once again it was written, "Out of Egypt, I have called My Son" (Matt. 2:13–15).

This magnificent relationship—Israel and Jesus—can be appreciated to a fascinating degree. There is a Biblical riddle in which the speaker asks, "Of whom am I talking?":

1. A biological miracle was performed on his mother so that he could be born.
2. He went off to Egypt, but was delivered back to the Promised Land.
3. He was called "the Son of God."
4. He was surrounded by enemies in Israel.
5. He was tormented and crucified.
6. He rose again to life on the third day.
7. He will reign for a thousand years.

It seems obvious that we are speaking here of the ministry of Jesus Christ, but in a remarkable way the entire list applies equally to the career of Israel:

1. The biological miracle of birth was in the aged Sarah delivering the child Isaac, through whom the promises were delivered to Israel.
2. Israel went to Egypt in its youth, just as we have explained, and was, of course, delivered back out to the Promised Land.
3. Israel was called "the Son of God" (Ex. 4:21–23; Hos. 11:1).
4. Back in Canaan, Israel was surrounded by enemies.
5. Israel was tormented constantly and finally "crucified" by the Romans in A.D. 70, when the Temple was destroyed and the Jews dispersed throughout the world.
6. Israel will rise again on the "third day" ("But, beloved, be not ignorant of this one thing, that one day is with the Lord as a thousand years, and a thousand years as one day"; II Pet.

3:8). Israel has been "dead"—as in Ezekiel's description of the dispersed nation as "dry bones"—for nearly two thousand years. But, according to prophecy, Israel will rise again to reign in the kingdom of the Lord.

7. The kingdom, also called the millennium, of course lasts a thousand years, and thus Israel and Jesus come together to reign in the final symbol.

MOSES AND JESUS

Moses is certainly one of the fundamental types of Christ in myriad aspects. Of course, we reviewed the Lord's prophecy that the Messiah would be "a prophet like Moses" (Deut. 18:15, 18).

Moses was chosen by God to be the deliverer of Israel from bondage to Pharaoh, and to bring them out of pagan Egypt to the Promised Land. Christ, likewise, was sent into the world to be the deliverer of the larger Chosen People, the worldwide believers, from slavery to sin and Satan and the pagan world system. When Moses was born, Pharaoh tried to have the promised deliverer eliminated by slaying the male infants, and, as we pointed out above, King Herod ordered the same thing in connection with prophecies of the birth of a new King in Bethlehem. Both Moses and Jesus escaped infanticide.

Moses offered to deliver Israel and to be their leader when he was forty years old, but the Hebrews refused to recognize him at that "first coming," as Stephen pointed out. It was not until forty years later, when Moses arrived back from Sinai and gave his second offer, that the Chosen People believed in him and acknowledged him as their deliverer. Likewise with Christ—at His first coming He was rejected. The Chosen People said they would "not have this man to reign over us" (Luke 19:14). But the prophets indicate that when the Messiah returns the second time, Israel will receive Him and welcome Him, and "all Israel shall be saved" (Rom. 11:26, Zech. 12:10, et al.).

During the time he was an outcast from his fellow Hebrews in Egypt, Moses married the daughter of Jethro, Zipporah. She was a Midianite, and thus a descendant of Ishmael, the son of Abraham by Hagar. She was part Semitic and part Gentile. During Christ's present exile from the nation of Israel, which has lasted over nineteen hundred years, He has taken a bride, the Church, which is part Jewish and part Gentile in composition—composed of all believers in Christ.

In his manifold capacities, Moses served Israel as prophet, priest, and King. He was a prophet exhorting his people to godliness and predicting things to come. He was a priest of the Tribe of Levi, constructing the Tabernacle of worship and interceding on behalf of Israel. He was a King, serving as the sole human authority over the twelve tribes, judging them and being their leader in all national matters. No one until the Messiah would again possess these three vital offices. The priests might be prophets, but not Kings; and no King was authorized to conduct priestly functions (II Chron. 26:16-20). But in the Messiah, all three offices converge again, as they did in Moses. Christ is the prophet par excellence, who revealed the essence of the law and predicted many events—some of which have already come to pass (the destruction of the Temple, for example, and the calling out of the Gentile believers). He is the Great High Priest, not descended from Levi but appointed directly by God, like the ancient friend of Abraham, Melchizedek of Salem. In His priestly role, He offered Himself as a complete sacrifice for the sins of the people, and is praying in priestly intercession for the believers now. His true power as King will be manifested when He returns to establish His millennial reign on earth.

The occasion of the long sojourn in the desert by the Hebrew nation before they entered the Promised Land (itself a type of the sojourn of the believer in the world before his ultimate victory), provided for many types. The most vital provision of God for His people, of course, was water (itself a type of the "living water" provided by Christ—John 4:10-13).

The Lord had told Moses to strike a large rock with his staff and a river of water would flow from it to quench the thirst of the people (as water flowed from the side of Christ, our Rock, when He was pierced with the spear). The Apostle Paul informs the Corinthian church that the rock which followed the people in the desert was a symbol of Christ; He is the Rock of Ages who has been struck and cleft for us in His death so that we may drink freely of the waters of everlasting life.

Also in the wilderness, the Chosen People encountered a judgment from God in the form of a great nest of poisonous snakes. They were attacked and there was no escape. When Moses prayed to the Lord, he was told to make a bronze serpent and hang it on a stick. If the people would merely look up at the bronze serpent, they would be healed of the effects of the venom and would live.

Some fifteen hundred years later, Jesus was to tell the Pharisee Nicodemus:

And as Moses lifted up the serpent in the wilderness, even so must the Son of man be lifted up: That whosoever believeth in him should not perish, but have eternal life. (John 3:14–15)

Thus, any man could look to the sacrificial death of Christ on the tree and be healed from Satan's venom of sin. Sin itself (the serpent, as in the Garden of Eden) was crucified with Christ.

JONAH AND THE RESURRECTION

During Christ's first coming, it was very clear to the Lord that the nation of Israel was not going to receive Him as Messiah. It was evident that the request of the religious leaders for Him to give them a sign that He was indeed the Promised One had become a kind of "cop-out." He informed them that the only sign they would get was the sign of the prophet Jonah:

Then certain of the scribes and of the Pharisees answered, saying, Master, we would see a sign from thee.

But He answered and said unto them, An evil and adulterous generation seeketh after a sign; and there shall no sign be given to it, but the sign of the prophet Jonas:

For as Jonas was three days and three nights in the whale's belly; so shall the Son of man be three days and three nights in the heart of the earth.

The men of Nineveh shall rise in judgment with this generation, and shall condemn it: because they repented at the
preaching of Jonas; and, behold, a greater than Jonas is here.
(Matt. 12:38–41)

Thus, just as Jonah was in the fish three days and nights and
then was regurgitated, so the earth, after three days and nights,
would give up the body of Jesus when He arose from the dead.

The story of Jonah, so often relegated to mere fable, is infinitely
more significant in the light of the Lord's remarks in the gospel;
especially in view of the fact that Jonah proceeded to take the saving message of the Lord immediately to the Gentiles (Nineveh).

THE TABERNACLE AND CHRIST

Whole books have been written on the infinite types of Christ
to be found in God's detailed instructions for the building of the
Tabernacle in the wilderness. God gave Moses the architectural
plans on Mount Sinai. The Tabernacle was a replica of the Tabernacle in heaven, which has existed and continues to exist for all
time. The Tabernacle showed Israel the proper way to worship
the living God, and was also a subtle and beautiful picture of the
Messiah (Heb. 8:1–5).

The bronze altar of sacrifice, where the animals were killed and
burned as prescribed offerings to the Lord, of course pointed to
the full and final sacrifice for sin that Christ would ultimately accomplish. The laver, or great bowl of water, where the priests
washed their hands and feet before entering the Tabernacle building, symbolizes the cleansing which each believer in Christ can experience as he lives in the Lord. In a very real sense, the follower
of Christ becomes a priest in His service, and he is to be purified
daily by the washing of the "water of the Word" of God (Eph.
5:26).

The Holy Place was an oblong room in the Tabernacle, which
contained just three pieces of furniture: The seven-branch oil
lampstand, or Menorah, was a type of Christ, "the Light of the
World"; the Table of Shewbread represents the Messiah as "the

Bread of Life"; the golden altar of incense, on which a special fragrant powder was burned, so that the smoke rose with the prayers of the priests on Israel's behalf, represents the intercession of Christ, "the Great High Priest," with the Father on our behalf (Heb. 7:25).

The second room of the Tabernacle was about half the size of the first and was called "the Holy of Holies." It contained the Ark of the Covenant—representing God's throne of grace and atonement. Once a year, on the Day of Atonement, the High Priest of Israel, and he alone, would enter this room and sprinkle the blood of the goat on the Ark, to atone for the sins of Israel. This is a type of Christ, who served as both the perfect High Priest (being sinless and wholly human), and also the perfect offering. He, as Priest, offered Himself as sacrifice to atone for the sins of the whole world, in the manner that the ancient High Priest atoned for the national sins of all Israel.

Between the two rooms was a six-inch thick veil, embroidered with beautiful and multicolored angelic figures. The veil separated the Holy of Holies—in effect, God's residence in the Tabernacle— from the Holy Place where the priests ministered. It is significant that the veil in the Temple was torn in half, top to bottom, when Christ died (Matt. 27:51). The implication was that the veil which had previously separated man from God had now been torn apart through the death of the Lord, and in this new age there is free access to the Throne of Grace; in effect, free access to God. Christ has made for us a new and living way (Heb. 9:1–8; 10:19–22).

The very materials out of which the Tabernacle was built were each a symbol. For example, gold (representing God) and wood (representing man) were laminated together in the Ark of the Covenant (thus representing Christ, God and man in one). Since man is wood in the Bible, the earthly occupation of the Lord is no accident; He was a carpenter, one who makes useful things of wood.

The two Temples which followed the Tabernacle were built in the same forms out of the same plans. Thus, when Christ entered the Temple in Jerusalem, He was, in effect, walking into a huge symbolic representation of Himself.

DAVID AND THE SON OF DAVID

King David was in many ways a type of his greater son, Jesus. One of the things the religious leaders of Israel—the Pharisees and scribes—frequently criticized the Lord about was His supposed breaking of the Sabbath, as they interpreted it. Jesus repeatedly refuted these unscriptural and tradition-filled interpretations of the Sabbath law. On one occasion, He and His men were pulling grains of wheat and eating them as they passed through a field on the Sabbath. The leaders rebuked them for this action, but Jesus responded by drawing a parallel between Himself and King David. David had been anointed as the new King by Samuel, but, of course, King Saul still had the power and had issued a death warrant on David, of whom he became insanely jealous. David escaped from Saul in Hebron, and found sanctuary in the Tabernacle at Shiloh. Nearly starving, David asked the priests of the Tabernacle if he and his men might eat the shewbread from the Tabernacle table, and, though it was consecrated for special purposes, the priests served them (I Sam. 21:1–6).

Jesus thus pointed out the greater law of the Sabbath; that the Sabbath was made for man, not man for the Sabbath, and that the Son of Man is Lord of the Sabbath (Matt. 12:1–8).

Thus, the Lord explained a type of Himself in David, who was rejected and maltreated by his nation Israel for a time, but was the Promised One of God and was provided for by God. David ultimately was, of course, recognized as the true King of Israel, as will be true also in the case of Christ.

THE KING OF PEACE AND
THE PRINCE OF PEACE

Solomon was also a type of Christ. His name means "peace," and he was the King of Peace. His reign was marked by a time of peaceful relations with the surrounding nations, and, at least at the beginning, of glory, beauty, and order. Jesus spoke of "Solomon in all his glory" (Matt. 6:29), but said that, "A greater than Solomon is here," referring to Himself.

When Christ returns to the earth and establishes His kingdom, He will raise the glory, beauty, and order of Solomon's reign to its ultimate fulfillment. He will bring total peace, righteousness, and holiness to the whole world, in a way that will show the reign of King Solomon to have been a mere shadow.

Comparing Himself to the ancients, the Lord made a stirring and ironic point before the rulers of the Chosen People:

> The queen of the south [Sheba] shall rise up in the judgment with this generation, and shall condemn it: for she came from the uttermost parts of the earth to hear the wisdom of Solomon; and, behold, a greater than Solomon is here. (Matt. 12:42)

THE GOOD SHEPHERD

One of the last of the Old Testament prophets, Zechariah, was commissioned by the Lord to conduct a one-man drama in which he would play the part of a faithful shepherd. After he served for a while, he was to ask for his pay. He would receive thirty pieces of silver, as the scenario went. This was considered an insult, rather than the proper wage, because it was the price of a common slave, according to the Law of Moses (Zech. 11:12). In contempt for such a poor remittance, the shepherd was to take the money and throw it into the Temple, to the potters (Zech. 11:13). Then the good shepherd would take his two staves and break them. The shepherd would be struck down and his sheep would be scattered (Zech. 13:7).

This drama of Zechariah turned out to be a wonderfully appropriate type of Christ, the Good Shepherd. In His first coming, He ministered to the flock of Israel. When it came time for the nation to determine His worth, the leaders paid the sum of thirty pieces of silver to Judas, to surrender Jesus to them (Matt. 26:15). Later, Judas, in his guilt, took the money and threw it at the priests in the Temple. Because it was blood money, they used it to purchase the potter's field, as a pauper's cemetery (Matt.

27:3–10). The Good Shepherd was struck down in death, and the sheep of Israel have been sadly scattered ever since. The staves of internal cohesion and external protection were broken, and the Romans were allowed to destroy Israel and Jerusalem and disperse the Jewish people throughout the world.

One day the Good Shepherd will gather His sheep back to Israel for national and spiritual redemption (Isa. 27:12–13).

TYPES OF THE BELIEVERS

The Old Testament contains types other than those portraying the person and work of Christ. There are types also of the Church, the called out body of believers during this age.

Eve is the first type of the Church in her relationship to Adam. When God presented the freshly created Eve to the first man, Adam exclaimed that she was "bone of his bones and flesh of his flesh." God responded, as they came together, that the two, man and woman, were now "one flesh":

And Adam said, This is now bone of my bones, and flesh of my flesh: she shall be called Woman, because she was taken out of Man.

Therefore shall a man leave his father and his mother, and shall cleave unto his wife: and they shall be one flesh. (Gen. 2:23–24)

The Apostle Paul saw in this primeval oneness of the first human parents an illustration of the oneness between Christ and the Church. The Church, like Eve, is betrothed to her husband, Christ. Paul refers to the Church actually as the "Bride of Christ," and the Church responds to Christ's self-sacrificing love in reverence, obedience, fidelity, and appreciation of the oneness that exists eternally between them:

For the husband is the head of the wife, even as Christ is the head of the church: and he is the saviour of the body.

Therefore as the church is subject unto Christ, so let the wives be to their own husbands in every thing.

Husbands, love your wives, even as Christ also loved the church, and gave himself for it. (Eph. 5:23–25)

In simplest form, Eve is a most elegant type of the Church: part of her husband's body, and also his bride.

THE TEMPLE AND THE CHURCH

While the worship and order of service in the early New Testament churches were more parallel to the contemporary Jewish synagogue than the Jerusalem Temple, the Church is referred to as "the Temple of God" in this age (Eph. 2:19–22). Just as the ancient Temple had its fine stones carefully cut at the quarry, and fitted into their proper places in the building, so all individual Christians are viewed as "living stones," cut and put together with divine craftsmanship into a spiritual Temple:

Now therefore ye are no more strangers and foreigners, but fellow-citizens with the saints, and of the household of God;

And are built upon the foundation of the apostles and prophets, Jesus Christ himself being the chief corner stone;

In whom all the building fitly framed together groweth unto an holy temple in the Lord:

In whom ye also are builded together for an habitation of God through the Spirit. (Eph. 2:19–22)

THE CAIN PEOPLE AND THE ABEL PEOPLE

The first two people born on earth are types of the two basic kinds of religious people from then on. Cain believed in God, of course, and wanted to honor Him in worship; but he brought the improper offering. As we explained in Part One, Cain brought produce from his field, while Abel brought the prescribed blood sacrifice to the Lord. Cain's resultant jealousy ended in murder (Gen. 4:3–8).

Cain is a type of the religious people of the world (not the atheists or agnostics), who believe they can earn God's approval by their own acts, works, or accomplishments. They bring to the Lord that which, in their own opinion, will please the Lord. Abel, on the other hand, represents those who realize they are sinners apart from God, and recognize their need for a mediator's blood to make atonement for them. In Abel's day, the lamb was correct; in this day, the Lamb of God has been provided (Heb. 11:4).

ISHMAEL AND ISAAC

The two sons of Abraham, Ishmael and Isaac, are types of Israel and the Church in this age. At Isaac's weaning party the teenager Ishmael taunted and ridiculed the infant since Ishmael was jealous of Isaac. The son of Hagar was merely a "son of the flesh," while Isaac was the "son of promise," as God had intended through Abraham and Sarah.

Ishmael, then, is a type of the Jewish people, the nation Israel in present days. Apart from their own Messiah, they still have a relationship to their father, Abraham, but only by the flesh and not in the spirit. The Church, on the other hand, composed of Gentile and Jewish believers in the Messiah, relates to Isaac, the son of promise. Jews and Gentiles who believe in Christ have inherited the marvelous spiritual blessings of their father, Abraham. But just as Ishmael taunted Isaac, Israel has taunted the true Church, saying that the believers in Christ have forsaken the law of Moses and are worshipping idols.

But the Lord has decreed that unbelieving Israel in the flesh cannot inherit eternal life along with the believing Church (Gal. 4:25–31).

Sadly, the tables have been turned throughout the centuries and some of the Church has taken on traditions of the flesh, much like Ishmael—such as becoming a state religion and having idols of wood and stone. Some sectors of the Church have actually become primary persecutors of Israel, and this is an ungodly and tragic turn of events.

But the true sons of Abraham by faith, who seek to be obedient to the God of Abraham and the Messiah, will have nothing to do with either the fleshly accretions or the persecution of Israel.

THE RED SEA AND BAPTISM

The crossing of the Red Sea by Israel with Moses is recognized as a type of baptism. The Israelites were dramatically separated from Egypt, and irrevocably identified with Moses the Deliverer as they went safely through the waters, having been redeemed by the blood of the Passover lamb. This is a type of the believer in Christ today, who has been redeemed by the blood of the Lamb of God and then submits to water baptism. Through this symbolic act, the believer indicates that he is cutting off the old life and identifying with Christ and His Church. Through immersion into the water, he portrays his own association with the death, burial, and resurrection of the Lord (I Cor. 10:1–2; Rom. 6:3–4).

The entire story of the redemption of the Israelites at the original Passover illustrates the life of the believer in Christ today in full. The Jews were saved by the blood of the lamb, emerged safely from the Red Sea, wandered in the wilderness, and ultimately entered the Promised Land. The believer in Christ likewise is saved by the blood of the Lamb; is immersed and brought forth from the water in baptism; sojourns in the wilderness (the world) in his earthly life; and ultimately progresses to the Promised Land—the victorious life in Christ, Heaven and the Kingdom of God.

Salvation in the New Testament is a repeat performance of what God had clearly illustrated previously in the Old Testament.

SINAI AND JERUSALEM

Two mountains dominate the Old Testament landscape: Mount Sinai and the Mountain of Jerusalem. According to the Apostle Paul, these two mountains are types of Law and Grace.

The law was given on Sinai, and the entire episode was marked by fire, earthquakes, and warnings that anyone besides Moses who approached the dreadful mountain of the Lord would die. Jerusalem, on the other hand, is pictured as the place of joy, worship, the sumptuous Temple, and God's grace. And this joy is particularly intensified in the future millennial Jerusalem.

Today, a person can place himself under the law and be chained to rules and regulations that he cannot keep. The law that in itself is good actually condemns us and kills us because we can't keep it. It is full of threats and rumblings and judgments like those of Sinai. The grace of God, however, is free and joyous, filled with the appeals and responses of mutual love and peace. The grace of God is like the happy streets of Jerusalem and the Levitical choirs in the ancient Temples during their finest days, and especially like the golden age of Jerusalem to come. When we cast ourselves gratefully on the grace and mercy of the Lord, we will find ourselves truly happy and serene, though the storms of life shriek and blow around us (Gal. 4:24–27).

It is fascinating to realize that when the law was given at Sinai, the idolatry with the golden calf caused the death of three thousand people (Ex. 32:28). When the Holy Spirit came to Jerusalem, exactly three thousand believed and were given eternal life (Acts 2:41). As the apostle pointed out meaningfully, "the letter killeth, but the spirit giveth life" (II Cor. 3:6).

FROM HERE TO ETERNITY

Men will be finding types in the treasure house of the Old Testament from now until the end of time. As we said at the beginning of this section, it would take volumes this size to give them all, if indeed all of them have been uncovered. The subtle and cryptic nuances of the Old Testament language—its types, symbols, and illustrations—greatly refresh and intensify what is taught in the New Testament. The types clearly demonstrate the fine old adage:

The New is in the Old concealed; the Old is in the New revealed.

The Old Testament was not only the Bible Jesus read. It is the Bible He perfectly fulfilled.